SACRAMENTS,
SIGNS AND
SYMBOLS

SACRAMENTS, SIGNS AND SYMBOLS

with
Essays on Related Topics

W. Norman Pittenger, S. T. M.

Instructor, Fellow and Tutor in the
General Theological Seminary
Lecturer in Religion, Columbia University

WILCOX & FOLLETT CO.
CHICAGO

Cloister

Books

For
Robert, Ruth and Marshal
who know and do
these things

CONTENTS

FOREWORD

It was the late Archbishop of Canterbury who remarked that of all the great religions Christianity is the most "materialistic," since (he pointed out) it is indisputable that its faith, worship and life are centered about the *incarnate* Lord who is the Eternal Word of God made *flesh*. Ever since I came across that profound observation of Dr. William Temple's, it has been in the back of my mind to write, one day, a book which would develop the idea more fully and in one particular direction—namely, the inextricable connection between the full historic Catholic faith built upon him who is the Word-made-flesh and the whole area of religious expression which in some theological writing has aptly been called "external religion."

That would mean a discussion of the significance of the ceremonial, physical, material and sacramental—in brief, things done and actions undertaken—which form so large and central a part of the religious life of the Christian who shares in the mainstream of historic Catholic faith and life. For me, it would mean particularly an approach to these matters from the position of one who is an Anglican and by that very fact a Catholic Christian.

At last the opportunity to think and write about these things has come to me; the present book, partial and inadequate as it is, summarizes the results of that thinking. It will be apparent that this book can make no claim beyond being a brief and perhaps suggestive study of a highly important matter. It attempts, in this suggestive fashion, to do something which—at least so far as my own reading has revealed—has not been done in recent times in the Episcopal Church.

It is of course apparent that the writer is an Episcopalian. But I would go on to say frankly that no other religion than Catholic Christianity as maintained in the Anglican Communion has ever been very meaningful for me, in any final sense. That confession will explain, perhaps, why I have written as I have. Yet it is my hope that whatever I have said is also reasonable and sound to one of my background and predilections. One must always distinguish between *how* one came to a certain position and *what may reasonably be said* for that position—the late Dr. Quick argued this point admirably in his little book *The Gospel of Divine Action*. My intention in this study of "external religion" has been to discuss *what may reasonably be said* for "the Catholic way." But it would, as I have indicated, be unfair to my readers to veil my own conviction that "the Catholic Way" is the *natural* way, the *best* way, and the way most calculated to give men an "experience" of Christian faith, worship and life that is most abundant and rewarding.

The line of argument is fairly direct. We begin with a sketch of historical Christianity as understood in the mainstream of the tradition and expressed in its worship, recognizing that it is a religion which is deeply rooted in man's materiality, finding God in an incarnational fashion, worshiping him sacramentally, employing natural and physical means for the expression of devotion and the stimulation of faith. We proceed to consider man's experience in the widest sense, and then the world itself as we experience it, noting that man is himself a body-mind complex while the world is a value-matter complex, in both of which purpose and meaning are mediated through sensible and physical realities. Against this background we study the nature of religion, historically and existentially, with a further discussion of Christianity to discover the place of the body in both. A final chapter has reflections on the relation of "spirituality" to "materiality," the place of sincerity in external practices and the element of personal appropriation.

To the first section of this book, dealing with the specific subject of "external religion," has been added a second section, composed of essays on related topics—all of them depending upon such a view of religion and Christianity as the first section indicates. Hence a certain repetition of ideas is found. It is hoped that their publication in the present form will answer the request of numerous readers who have asked that these essays, most of them previously published in a different form in periodicals, be made available in book-form. For permission to reprint, in part or entirely, the material in the second section, and certain paragraphs in the first, the author is grateful to the editors of *The Living Church*, *The Christian Century*, *Christendom* and *The Anglican Theological Review*.

W. NORMAN PITTENGER

Chelsea Square,
New York City

PART ONE

Sacraments, Signs and Symbols

1. THE FACE OF HISTORICAL CHRISTIANITY

The "Man from Mars" has been somewhat over-worked, but he has a certain usefulness. So we shall begin this study of the use and meaning of sacraments, signs and symbols in historical Christianity by invoking his presence with us. He landed here in this very year of grace, after several earlier trips to this weird planet on which men live. We requested him to undertake a tour of the various Christian bodies which are to be found in the world today. He agreed to make the expedition and has just now returned. We ask him to describe to us what a man from another planet sees while wandering about the earth. He replies:

"I discovered once again the fact that I have noted on my earlier visits. I find that most of the people who are called Christian seem to act in pretty much the same fashion through the centuries, and on this particular and extensive trip, I find that they also do pretty much the same sort of thing all over the world. You ask me to describe their manner of worship and their life of devotion, so far as I can discover them. That is not difficult to do—the describing of them, I mean. In fact, I could put it in very few words: these Christian people do things with their bodies which they seem to think have much importance and which they evidently believe have some close relationship to what goes on in their souls and minds.

"What do I mean by that? Something like this —that everywhere I go I find that most of the people

1

who call themselves Christian go periodically to buildings which are called churches. There they hold their 'services of worship.' In these they stand or sit or kneel. They seem to do these things at certain prescribed times during the 'service,' varying their posture according to rules which have evidently been devised for this purpose. They make gestures of one sort or another; sometimes they beat their breasts, sometimes they bow low, sometimes they make a rapid kneeling and rising which they call 'a genuflexion'; sometimes they make a sign on their bodies, like a cross.

"Their leaders in worship—the people whom they call priests—also make such gesticulations and indulge in such actions. They bow and kneel and stand and beat their breasts and make signs of various kinds over the worshiper or over objects usually placed on a table called an altar but sometimes placed elsewhere. They wear special and rather formalized garments; sometimes these are very brightly colored and sometimes black or white. They speak aloud—and so do the people themselves who are present in the building and are what is known as the congregation. Most often in speaking they are using words taken from books which have come down to them, so they say, from an earlier age. Now and again, they read selections from a great volume called 'The Holy Scriptures'; frequently they employ the form of words found in prayer books and other volumes. There is singing by the people, too, as well as music by choirs and on instruments such as an organ. Sometimes the singing is very formal and precise, according to a rule; sometimes it is fairly free and rather more like the songs which earth-folk sing outside the place of worship.

"The buildings for worship are sometimes great

edifices, sometimes little ones, but always they are fitted with the same kind of ornaments and furniture. There are altars and shrines and pictures and statues and candles and decoration—often it is quite simple, sometimes it is very elaborate. The windows of the churches are frequently, if not always, filled with colored glass which sometimes is so arranged that figures of men and women and children are represented. There are fragrant and colorful flowers placed here and there about the building. Nor is the odor of flowers the only odor which greets one's nostrils. In many of the churches incense is burned at one time or another so that the whole building is filled with a pungent but sweet smell.

"The leaders, with their singers and their assistants sometimes walk about the building, frequently in great processions, carrying colored banners and candles, wearing rich and ornate garments, singing as they go—either the musical compositions which are called hymns, or shorter and more terse affairs called litanies, in which prayers are repeated and responses made by people and choir.

"It is all very active and colorful, very much a matter of bodily movement and word. In fact it seems to me that most of the Christian religion that I have seen is expressed in some fashion by the use of the body, either by its motions or by something which appeals to the senses of sight, hearing, touch, taste or smell. And I must not forget to mention one other thing, which seems to be very important to these Christians as the clue to all their worship. In services much is said about eating and drinking what appears to be bread and wine but which they call 'body' and 'blood,' and which is linked in their faith with the one whom they call their 'Lord' and describe as 'God-Man.' It is around that chief act of worship that there revolve the many others in which water, oils and lights are used. It is in a sense a materialistic business. If you come down to it, Christianity, I should say, is a pretty definite bodily way of being religious."

So far the Man from Mars.

He has been describing, as you and I well know, historic Catholic worship, whether that be found among the Eastern Orthodox or Roman Catholics or Episcopalians, all over the world. Evidently the Man from Mars feels that this is the typical form of all Christian worship. Nor is he in error on this point. For, you recall, he has made other visits to the earth, and doubtless on these visits he travelled about among Christians, too, and saw on those occasions what was, in effect, the same thing that he saw on today's visit. With minor variations, it has always been in essential matters the same. So, his description is quite accurate.

Even if he had happened to mention the group of Christian believers, rather numerous in certain parts of the world (as in North America, above the Mexican border; or in certain parts of Europe, north of the Alps), who in their worship do not follow so fully the pattern which he outlined, he would still be obliged in describing them to say much the same sort of thing about them as he said about the more strictly "Catholic communions." For while the Protestant believers have omitted or neglected certain of the actions and signs which he mentioned, they are obliged to use many of them whether they desire to do so or not, simply by the fact that these Christians also are men with bodies. The Man from Mars knows whereof he speaks. He is describing Christianity as it really is, even if some might wish that it were not that way.

Now let us suppose that our unearthly visitor were also admitted into the private devotions of Christian folk. Let us ask him what he has found in that secret place of religious life and worship. He replies:

"About the same kind of thing that I found in the public services of Christians. These Christian people seem always to be expressing their religion in an external fashion. Even the simplest of them kneel now and again, or at least bow their heads and close their eyes. They tend to engage in small acts of devotion like making the sign of the cross over their bodies; they beat their breasts in private as well as in public; they even go about lighting candles and placing flowers before statues or pictures. In fact, they seem to make a great deal of such actions, which must signify something quite important to them. They do other things, too. They observe periods of abstaining from food or certain kinds of food. Daily they read selections from their holy book. They take for their own use certain forms of prayer from other volumes which they find convenient for the purpose. Most of them go privately now and again to kneel in a church beside one of their priests and tell in his presence the things that weigh on their hearts and consciences; all of them so far as I have been able to observe, do something or other like this in public worship to express their sense of wrong-doing. I should say that for these Christians—of course more with one man than with another—the body plays a central part in their private religion as well as in their public religion."

"That is very interesting," we reply. "What then do you make of it all?"

To which he answers, "At least this: that religion somehow seems naturally expressed in that fashion for these people. After all, they are men with bodies as well as souls and minds; I cannot but feel that it is impossible for men to do much with their souls or minds if they leave their bodies out of the picture. Of course Mars may be different from your planet, but out there we know perfectly well that all of our thinking, feeling, loving and acting is necessarily compounded of mind and body. I fancy it is the same with men on the earth. Therefore, I am not at all surprised that the religion of Christians is built up in exactly that manner. And I might add another point. These Christian folk are always talking about the chief article in their religion as being the conviction that the Almighty God once dwelt uniquely in their midst in human form. They say that God has lived a human life, and they claim that it is the central affirmation of Christianity that by doing this even to the death he has (to use their own phrase) 'saved them.' Since they say this, it would seem to me that their own religion, being based on what is really a belief in God's use of physical and material things like a human body, demands that they should act as they do. It is very logical. It is obviously reasonable for people who believe as they do to act as they do. For myself, I think it corresponds to the logic of human living."

Now the Man from Mars has to hurry off to catch his airship which will carry him to the red planet that is his home. So we take leave of him with an expression of gratitude for his friendly interest, and we turn to the perhaps less exciting task of coming to an understanding of the phenomenon which his observation has disclosed. If this is Christianity, what can be said for it? What about these sacraments, signs, symbols—this bodily expression of religion? Christianity has looked like this for a long time now. It looks like this at the moment of writing—from the Christmas celebration of the Divine Liturgy in Moscow to the Pope's Mass at St. Peter's in Rome; from Westminister Cathedral in London, which is Roman Catholic, to Westminister Abbey, which is Anglican; from St. Mary the Virgin, Times Square, New York, to some little mission church in the hills of South Dakota, where the Episcopal Church has a priest; from the lovely Hogalid Church in Stockholm to a Roman Catholic cathedral in South America; from Ireland to India and from Germany to New Guinea. Yes, even in circles called "Protestant" there is a marked approximation—now in greater degree, now in less—to this kind of religion. Among Protestants, notably, as the years roll by and the members of these bodies return to the tradition of their own founders or go forward to seek ways of making their particular version of the Christian faith a vital reality to their members, there is more and more "external religion." Quakers, too, are within the circle for they have places of meeting, words spoken, positions taken, times and seasons, sometimes music, special costumes and particular modes of speech. What is to be said concerning all this, then? Surely we are obliged to consider seriously this question of "external religion."

The fact is that "material" symbols and signs of all sorts have been shown to be a central and indispensable element in historical Christianity. This is not only true of "Catholic" Christianity; it is true of Christianity as a whole. It is, of course, much more obviously true of the "Catholic" type of Christianity. A visit to any Roman Catholic, Eastern Orthodox or Anglican parish church or cathedral will convince one of that. It is also true that a certain kind of mind insists that any and every use of such material signs and representations is profoundly wrong. Sometimes the word of condemnation is that it is "superstition"; sometimes it is said to be "unspiritual."

The succeeding chapters, while not attempting to deal specifically with these particular words or even with these particular charges, will perhaps do something by way of an answer in that they will attempt to show the significance and value of that which by these words is meant to be condemned. But nowadays it is quite plain that the condemnation is rather more tempered than in an earlier age. Indeed, it may be said that one of the most remarkable spectacles of our own time is the increasing willingness on the part of Protestant leaders and the increasing desire on the part of Protestant laymen to introduce and employ in their worship and devotion more of the traditional "sacred signs"—to use one of the classical descriptions of external religious observance. It would be a waste of space to quote as extensively as one might from the growing Protestant literature which has something to say on this very subject. The literature is too large. It must suffice simply to mention half a dozen useful books by Protestant leaders, books which are devoted largely, if not entirely, to the matter: W. L. Sperry, *Reality in Worship;* Van Ogden Vogt, *Modern Worship;* F. R. Webber, *Church Symbolism;* James Bissett Pratt, *The Religious Consciousness;* C. H. Heimrath, *Genius of Public Worship;* S. F. Brenner, *Way of Worship.*

In each of these works, concerned as they all are with a discussion of the question of the Christian Church's devotion and worship as understood by admittedly Protestant writers, there is ample treatment and generous recognition of symbols, signs, sacraments. And a visit to the newer buildings in which Protestant worship is carried on discloses that the theoretical approval in books is now implemented in actual practice architecturally and in the services of worship themselves. Not so much has been done in the development of external expression in private religious practice, but even in this field some few books have come to the public which are not without significance—as, for instance, Roger Hazelton's *Root and Flower of Prayer* and Douglas Steere's *Prayer and Devotion*. Something is afoot in Protestant circles in the matter of "externality in religion."

It is commonplace, of course, that the non-Christian religions have abounded in such manifestations of the religious spirit. From the primitive savages, whose religious observances have been so strikingly and interestingly portrayed in Marett's *Sacraments of Simple Folk*, straight up to the worship in the Hindu temple—non-congregational as it is—the use of some sort of representations, either in action or in symbol or in both, is always to be found. Professor Pratt *(Can We Keep the Faith?* page 44) mentions such objects as "the crescent, the trident, the stupa, the sky-pointing spire, the image of Vishnu, the Shiva lingam, the lotus, the mystic rose, the vine, the marble Buddha, deep in contemplation," as typical of the use of symbolic representations amongst non-Christians . . . and he is not concerned in this particular context with the need to give references to the symbolic and meaningful *actions* of the worshipers or devotees. If one were particularly interested in the latter, one could compile an even longer list. The suggestion is made by Professor Pratt that these symbols in religious practice have the function "in an indirect fashion and through the power of association, to rouse in the listener the state of mind which we have or which we wish to have set up in him, or to induce it in ourselves." Although this explanation of function is by no means entirely adequate, it is *part* of the truth, as we shall see; our point at the moment, however, is to indicate that some such idea appears to be connatural with all high religion as well as with the most primitive and "undeveloped" religion.

The universality both in presence and in employment of such objects and actions is certainly highly impressive. This is not the place to say whether or not they are justified by sound reasons of whatever sort. It is the *fact* merely which we are concerned to emphasize—the fact that something done by the body or appearing to the bodily senses has its fundamental place in the actual situation of man as a religious animal.

We should admit at once, of course, that the use of the sacrament-sign-symbol complex may lead to serious abuses, and that this has happened time and again in the history of religion. Today, likewise, there are doubtless grave dangers and even terrible abuses to be noted. Sometimes the symbols or actions are positively immoral, at least to *our* thought —and here we are referring to some of the practices found not only among primitive savages "in darkest Africa" but also among the civilized believers in the highly developed religions of India. Even among Christians there has often been abuse, very grave abuse, although it would be invidious and unnecessary to indulge in a catalog of the lapses from sound and reasonable practice. The point is not that error may and frequently *does* follow in the train of the "materiality" of much religion with the consequence that this "materiality" becomes or may become a sheer materialism. The point is that there seems to be an ineradicable and indeed essential drive in man as a religious being to express himself in these ways, even when and even though he recognizes that "the practice may lead to abuses." The defense must be made—and will be made, if obliquely, at a later moment—that as St. Thomas Aquinas remarked in another connection, *abusus non tollit usum*. The fact that something may be seriously *misused* does not deny or render unseemly its *proper use*. In any case, the plain truth remains that man is inclined to such ways of expressing himself religiously. It would appear the part of wisdom to accept the fact as it is and see what we can make of it. It is far too real a fact to be dismissed as nothing more than an unhappy lapse.

Indeed it seems that these ways of behaving are inseparably and necesarily related to the nature of man as the animal who is strangely marked by that "affinity with the Transcendent," which Kierkegaard, among others, has singled out as the sign of high religion. It was this kind of thing, indeed, that the Man from Mars was telling about in the words which we put in his mouth a few pages back. But because the Man from Mars was not a Christian and only an outside observer, he could not express what was going on in Christian public worship or in Christian private devotion with that depth of insight and warmth of understanding which would have made the description come alive to his Christian hearers. He could not use the Christian *words*— words which themselves are symbols, as Professor Urban has so convincingly argued in his treatment of religion in *Language and Reality* (pages 580-582), and which are utterly necessary for *any* discussion of *any* sort. This point, incidentally, is not to be overlooked, although we shall not need to dwell upon it since everyone nowadays will admit that all our verbalism is of the nature of symbolical expression. This is true of religious verbalism *a fortiori*. The Man from Mars was at an unhappy disadvantage in that he did not know and hence could not use those significant words such as "heavenly Father," "Jesus Christ our Lord," "the Body and Blood of Christ," "salvation," "miserable sinner," *etc.*, which are inevitable and invaluable in any attempt at more than the most superficial description either of Christian public worship or private devotion.

One could go on at considerable length on this point. But there can be no doubt whatever about the bodily expressions and impressions which take a central place in the religious life of the Christian and especially in him who is a sharer in the Catholic way. To the question "whether soul helps body more than body soul" he would probably have to answer that he could not say anything beyond the simple assertion that both of these play their genuine part in his religion. If he were "an intellectual"—to use our current lingo—he would likely go on to remark that since he, like all men, is a body-soul complex himself, it is the inevitable fact that his religion and his religious practice involve both soul and body, and that it is impossible to tell where one stops and the other begins, or how much influence there is either way.

Such a fashion of stating it will make a satisfactory starting-place for our next inquiry, which concerns the nature of man himself. To that we shall proceed in the following chapter.

2. MAN AS AN AMPHIBIAN

Many of us feel that Baron Friedrich von Hügel was the wisest, most balanced and most profound writer on religious subjects in this century. On the subject under consideration in this chapter, von Hügel had much to say. In fact, his entire philosophy of religion, so far as its anthropology was concerned, was built upon the two-fold nature of man and his world. In one of his essays, for instance, he has occasion to remark *(Essays & Addresses,* II p. 62) : "As a matter of simple fact we nowhere find, as a constituent of our own human life and nature (except we ourselves make abstractions) *pure* spirit, or *pure* body, or a *purely* spiritual or *purely* bodily act. But everywhere we only find spirit awakened by, and in its turn awakening, checking, impelling, spiritualizing body; and body furnishing such awakening, material friction, medium of expression and of appeal, yet also obstruction and deflection, to spirit."

Nor does von Hügel speak alone in this matter. The witnesses to the truth about which he is testifying stretch from Aristotle through St. Thomas Aquinas to William James. We might cite Aristotelian realism in the theory of knowledge. The insistence of St. Thomas that "nothing is in the mind which is not first in the senses" need hardly be mentioned. The Jamesian premise, as given in *Psychology (Briefer Course* p. 6), is the "correlation of brain-states with mind-states." All bear out von Hügel's main contention. To use the phrase employed on one occasion and in this connection by Miss

Evelyn Underhill, man is an "amphibian."

Obviously man is an animal, and he is, in many respects, like the other members of the animal kingdom. But he differs from the rest in the respect of capacity for thought; he is possessed of "a rational nature." Yet he is "conditioned," as the psychologists would put it, by the observable fact that he must receive the *material* for his thinking, must indeed *do* his thinking, by means of bodily instruments, even if the supreme instrument be the highly involved and sophisticated one of the human brain. This is not to *equate* thinking with certain convolutions of the grey cells in the brain; it is, as James said, to *correlate* them. It is not to say that the music played by the violin is nothing other than the catgut which in certain fact constitutes the strings; it is to say that no violin music is possible, so far as we are aware, without the instrumental employment of those strings.

Man's body, in truth, is a very thoroughly developed means whereby he acts and wherein he acts. Man's body is also a means whereby he receives impressions and is able to know whatever it is that he does know. It is *possible* that there are other means of knowing—non-sensory means. Dr. Rhine's book *Extra-Sensory Perception* discusses the subject at some length. But of these we know very little indeed, despite the mass of evidence Dr. Rhine has accumulated. It is not only wisdom but commonsense to insist upon some kind of check which sensible perception provides on the too ready use (by many writers) of vague terms like "intuition" and "insight." The problem of the relation of the *mind which knows* to the *body by which it knows* is a very complicated one. It is not for us at this point to attempt to settle it. However, there is no doubt about one thing: it is quite clear that ordinary human experience makes the simple observation that the body is an inalienable and essential element in the functioning of the human personality, and that man himself, as an existential personality, is the "wedding" of

> ... two worlds immense
> Of spirit and of sense.

As far back as infancy, the human animal learns chiefly through his bodily experiences. Things, persons, one sort of happening or another "bumps" up against him, so to say. It is by responding to these insistent pressures and by relating them one to another in his total organism that he comes to that place or point of experience where it is possible for him to make a "rational" account both of them and of life as he is obliged to live it. It is in, through, with and under his physical experiences that his mental processes begin to operate, come to maturity and start to react upon his bodily actions so that the latter may *express* what initially they received, worked upon, ordered and related when taken into the organism as *impressions*.

So it is that the body serves not only as the recipient of stimuli but also as the agent *for reaction and for action*. We emphasize the latter point especially since it appears that some have felt that all man can do is to *react* to stimuli, whereas the truth of experience is that we can initiate a series of events in the physical world, both the world of our own bodies and the world that exists externally to us. The attempt to reduce all human behavior to a solely responsive movement without any initiating capacity whatsoever would make man but an automaton, a view which is logically self-condemned for it eviscerates truth of meaning and destroys the very hypothesis which it advocates. The body is both the *impressive* and *expressive* agent for the total human personality while the "engineer" of the personality is the *rationality* of the man, his reason. In the scholastic definition, man is called "an individual substance of a rational nature." In another idiom, he has been described as an animal who thinks and because he thinks he is therefore *sui generis* and different from the other animals for whom thinking is not the specific quality or *differentia*.

But one important fact is often overlooked in this scholastic account of man. That is the place of the emotional life in man's total pattern. While it is true that man as man is a rational animal and while it must also be taken for granted, indeed frequently insisted upon, that he functions through his body when he functions at all, it is not so regularly recognized that part of man's bodily functioning, and therefore an essential element in the correct understanding of what is involved in his rationality, is that side of his total personality which responds to the external world or which goes out to the external world in terms of "feeling-tone." Man does say, over and over again, as he responds to the pressures of experience, something like "I enjoy it," "it satisfies my feelings," or their contrary. Here is a very genuine part of human living, and a part which we neglect at our peril. Even more serious is the tendency of the scholastic account to overlook the glandular, visceral, in general the organic, basis of the emotional life of men. It is as if man could somehow be seen as a mind inhabiting and using an "ideal" body from which had been removed all that makes it warmly and distinctively bodily. But that this is not

the truth our simplest experiences of perception, not
to mention our higher experiences of human fellowship, will make plain. I can *never* dissociate myself,
either as a body or as a thinking being, from the
reality of appreciation, depreciation, liking, dislik-
ing, desiring strongly or strongly disapproving. As
a man I am emotionally constituted.

Furthermore, as a man compound of body and
soul each of us dwells in community. That is to say,
our experiencing of life is largely socially prepared
and socially given. That which we know is mediated
to us to a very considerable degree through our
"contacts" with other men, and not least through our
participation in the social tradition of which willy-
nilly we are a part. Precisely as it is impossible to
envisage man without a body, so it is impossible to
envisage him without sociality. The "Good Man
Friday" who lives alone, with never a human relationship, is not truly a man, although he is, of course,
human by the proper philosophical definition. However that definition may be, he is not human in the
truest sense of the term, which means also to be a
member of, a sharer in, and a recipient of life *from*
as well as a giver of life *to* a community in which he
takes a significant place.

The consequence of this "social conditionedness"
of man is that he must not only *express* himself actually and also receive his *impressions* of the world
through bodily media; he must also be dependent on
the social environment for his perceptions of fact
and idea. He can no more get away from society
than he can get out of his own skin. His society
may be friendly to him or alien to him; none the less,
he depends upon it. He may dislike his life in the
community, or he may accept it gladly and freely; he
cannot escape it. The institutions of corporate hu-

man existence are part of the total framework of human life.

It is interesting and significant, in fact, that as we speak of man's physical vehicle as his *corporeal* nature, so we use the same Latin root to describe his social vehicle: it is man in his *corporate* nature. This is an indication that the insight of the race has understood that in one sense anyway society is, so to put it, an extension of man's "embodiedness." It is not at all an accident; it is essential to man as the strange amphibian being that he is.

Nothing has brought this so clearly home to us in recent years as the tremendous upsurge of racism and the emphasis on the *volk* and the "state." Mr. J. W. Harvey in the Autumn 1944 number of the English journal, *Philosophy,* comes to our assistance at this point. He indicates that the Nazi party philosophy may have had much about it that was thoroughly vicious, but it did at least recognize something which western democracies had tended to forget in their emphasis on "rugged individualism" —namely, the reality of man's intimate inter-penetrating appreciative relationship with his fellows in a common sociality. It is extraordinary, to say the least, to note that when it is so strikingly, not to say stridently, thrust before their eyes, many are not able to see the truth because its denial has given rise to a reaction in a perverse over-emphasis of the genuine reality.

However this may be, we may assume that it will be granted by the discerning observer of human society and the critical student of his own life that, according to any balanced understanding of man, he is a body-mind who is also a *society*-body-mind. By this we mean, in summary statement, that it is exactly in the instrumentality of the physical body and

of the social environment that man as mind is able
to act and that man as mind is acted upon and stim-
ulated to act for himself.

Still another point which needs attention, but
which has frequently been overlooked, is that in this
total picture of man as society-body-mind complex,
the prevenient action, i.e., the *earliest initiating step*
towards the rich interplay between mind, body and
society, comes, epistemologically speaking, from the
outside. Man, as it were, is a focus for influences
and drives which play upon him. It has even been
suggested that his development is not unlike that
of the eye—the rays of the sun, beating down upon
an organism, cause an irritation which in turn un-
dergoes a considerable development. Presently the
result is the eye which is the seeing-agent of the
whole organism. So, it has been urged, man is provoked into rationality—or perhaps better put his
latest rationality, is provoked into open activity—by
the play of the outside world upon him through his
senses. This priority, first of the external world
and then of the sense-instruments which convey
that world into man's mind, is the only guarantee which we possess of the being of a non-
human world at all. Furthermore, it is the criterion
which we consciously or unconsciously employ when
we endeavor to discriminate among our ideas and arrange them so that in greater or less degree they
accord with what we feel "to be really there."

Now it is not necessary—indeed it would be absurd—to suggest that the objects of our experience
are somehow introduced in their own proper and
essential reality into our minds through the instrumentality of the senses. Much wiser is the view associated with St. Thomas Aquinas and those who
after him have followed in the line of a critical re-

alistic epistemology. Here it is asserted that the *intelligible species* of the object enters into or is actually received into the mind in the act of knowing. The object known has about it "the possibility," or even better "the capacity," of being apprehended by mind through sensory vehicles of perception. This object is then by means of this "species" directly grasped and seized by the mind. But it is not grasped and seized without any mediation. The mind reaches out, so to say, and centers upon one or another datum, somewhat as a searchlight plays about the landscape and picks now this and now that spot for the observer to notice. Once the spot has been picked or the datum selected, the object or reality *is* grasped and known. Yet it is not grasped and known without the employment of an instrument. The searchlight must function if the spot on the landscape is to be studied; likewise, it is necessary that the senses operate if the datum is to be grasped.

Such a view of man as an amphibian is sheer common-sense. As it has often been remarked, it is only when sophisticated thinkers begin to work on the deliverances of sheer experience that a realistic epistemology is denied. Furthermore, it is the strange truth that when the very same thinkers are not engaged in their philosophizing they are *obliged* to act precisely upon the same terms and in precisely the same fashion as those who accept a critical realism. Nobody was ever an idealist, epistemologically speaking, in his day-by-day living. He always treats his wife, his child, his friends, his arm-chair, his lamb-chop, his pencil, as more than a construct of the mind. These things are there, and wisely or unwisely he trusts his sense experience when it tells him that they *are* there.

Let us consider, from another point of view, the

way in which all of our knowledge, even of so-called
spiritual values, is conveyed to us through the instrumentality of our senses. We say, for example,
that we know our friend John is here with us in the
room. But how do we know it? We know it because we can see him with our eyes, even if they be
somewhat imperfect in their focusing and not the
perfectly accurate organ of vision that they might
be. We can hear his voice and we are obliged to
use our ears if we are to do this. We can take his
hand in greeting, or put our arm around his shoulder
in affectionate interest, yet these are sense activities.
No matter how we are approached by him, our relationship is mediated by sense impressions. On the
other hand, when *we* move towards him, in our poor
human attempts to understand his thoughts or in
our yearnings to express our affection and concern
for him, we must do this through our eyes, ears,
hands—through our bodily instrument. There is no
other way. So long as we remain men, we approach
the world through the body or we do not approach
it at all. And so long as we remain men, we receive
impressions from the world through the body, or we
do not receive them at all.

An interesting instance which proves the contention is the case of Miss Helen Keller. She lacks
many of the senses which ordinary mortals possess.
Yet she is herself clear that it is through sense, by
means of a "feeling" more generally diffused
throughout her body than localized in particular
senses (some of which she does not have for her use),
that she knows others, is aware of their presence and
can enter into rapport with them. Dr. Rhine's experiments in what he calls "extra-sensory perception" are probably quite valid so far as they go, but
in calling them by that name he seems to have begged

the question. It is not at all unlikely, and in fact it seems the most likely explanation, that the vibrations which proceed from mind to mind, but which are in fact given forth from mind through body, are not *extra-sensory* at all, but are on the contrary only more refined and delicate physical responses than those which are habitual with us most of the time. The "Dunninger audiences," where the facts about other's lives and experiences are apparently known to the so-called "brain expert," are very likely to be explained in a similar fashion. At least this is a possible way of understanding them. But even if there are rare instances in which by some way of direct perception, without immediate sense instrumentality, something is known of another's thought, this does not mean that the general run of humanity, most of the time and in most of the situations in which men find themselves, are not dependent upon their senses for that which they know and think.

Now there is one point to be made and made as plainly as possible. As William James remarks in his *Psychology*, let not this view be taken for materialism. We have not denied either the reality of mind or the supreme fact that in its own right it can function properly and initiate action. Mind is *not* an epiphenomenon, in Huxley's or Clifford's phrase. It is not like the steam from the locomotive, which has no genuine part to play in making the engine go down the tracks. It is a *real* factor, the *central* factor, the *determining* factor in man. But it is mind *in body*, mind "conditioned by" body, mind expressing itself and receiving its knowledge in and through the body, which is the significant truth. The reality of some direct knowledge of another, which may come as a sort of "intuition," and similarly the reality of our capacity to give ourselves directly to another, are in no sense contradictory of this truth. Rather they indicate that it is possible for two total personalities to meet and live together in the deepest level of their being, through their bodily apprehensions, necessarily, but yet also in the very essential being of their inner lives.

Baron von Hügel once remarked that he kissed his baby because he loved it, while he loved it more because he kissed it. So it is in all of our knowledge of one another. We know each other because we see, hear, touch each other; but the very fact of our sensible understanding of each other deepens the knowledge which itself inaugurates. It is absurd to say that even in what purport to be entirely "spiritual" relationships, there is no physical substratum. This does not suggest that there is no relationship which is not grossly physical, of course. It does mean that even in our most "elevated" and "spiritual" contacts, it is the *thereness* of the other, our perception of him through our senses, which makes the relationship possible and which is the condition of our maintaining it in our lives. Aldous Huxley has pointed out that the one thing which is important about a body is that "it is indubitably there." And one's relations with others would dissolve into sheer vapor if there were not that embodied *thereness*.

Thus it is, too, with our knowledge of the natural world. We may put together in a thoroughly erroneous fashion the material received through our sense-impressions. There is no need to contend that we always know infallibly, despite the long insistence by the scholastics that the senses as such cannot err. But even the scholastics were obliged to modify their epistemological realism in the direction of a sound criticism of the deliverances of the senses. Our senses deliver to us what they apprehend to be there,

what they feel or see or hear or smell, or what they
grasp in a "kinaesthetic" fashion. How this gets put
together in our minds is another matter. On the
other hand it is useless to deny that there is no
ordinary contact with the external world excepting
in this fashion. We must seek, by comparison with
others, by criticism of new sensations in the light of
of older and habitual ones, by the fruitfulness and
rewarding development of our understanding, to get
the thing straight, so to say. It is not otherwise as
we move out towards our world. Here too our physical instrument may not be adequate to express, indeed never could be adequate to express, yet it is
essential for the expression.

If I wish "to get myself across," I must say
words, I must look at someone, I must grasp a hand,
or I must kiss the beloved one. Sometimes the denial
of this truth of bodily instrumentality can lead to
absurd conclusions. It might imply that one should
say to his friend, "I like you so much that I won't
grasp your hand"; or to one's lover, "I love you so
dearly that I shall not kiss you." The unnaturalness
and inhumanity of such actions at once condemn
them. But we must be prepared to carry the principle even farther, and see how it applies in every
area of our knowing and conscious life. In the last
resort, as we have seen William James insisted, even
purely interior thought is dependent upon the grey-
matter of the brain. To think accurately means,
therefore, to think accurately *with the brain*, not in
some discarnate fashion without the brain or extra-
cerebrally.

St. Thomas Aquinas has expressed one side of
this truth extremely well when he writes, "By means
of external signs, whether of words or deeds, the
human mind is moved as regards apprehension and

consequently also as regards the affections." *(Summa Theologica II. 83.12.)* He also stated the other side along with it, when after having remarked that "it is connatural to us to proceed from the sensible to the intelligible," *(S.T.II. 84.2)* he goes on to say, "The mode befitting to man is that he should employ sensible signs in order to signify anything, because he derives his knowledge from sensibles," *(S.T.II.85.1)* The "common-sense" of the Angelic Doctor has always been a matter of comment; here it is very clearly manifest.

In conclusion, then, we have come to the recognition that man is an amphibious being, who may be called a soul or mind inhabiting a body, or a body indwelt by a mind or soul, but who more satisfactorily should be called a complex soul-body or mind-body organism. In man, so conceived, the distinctive feature is his rationality or mind. This marks him out from the other animals. However, the fact that he is so endowed does not imply that he can slip out of his body and think and act as if he were not possessed of it. Such a notion has well been termed by M. Jacques Maritain: "angelism." It is quite as bad, from its side, as the opposite error which would regard man as *nothing but* body.

We have not been concerned, however, to stress the error of "corporealism" (as we may call it), nor to point out the terrible dangers to which it leads. Our reason for this is very simple: when religious folk, or those who are discussing religion, are in question, *their* danger is usually never in the direction of over-estimating the body. Rather, it is in the direction of under-estimating it, and either saying or wishing that man were not so constituted. But the sound attitude is one well-expressed in a hymn by Percy Dearmer, in which he speaks of "the wonder and weakness of flesh." It is a glorious and wonderful thing that the human body is here both as the expressive medium for mind and also as the receiving instrument for mind. Yet there is a weakness about the flesh or body, since (first) it may deceive us in its deliverances about the world, life and reality unless we accept these critically, *i.e.*, rationally, and (secondly) it is always inadequate to "get us across" . . . for man is greater than his body, and there is always a *more* in him, an unplumbed depth of being which no medium can do other than convey imperfectly and brokenly. Man's *embodiedness* is both his "tragedy and grandeur" (to use words of Pascal's in another connection) but it is an inescapable fact. In religion, as everywhere else in life, we do well to accept the facts, humbly and gratefully. We certainly need not wish them otherwise, and we are wiser when we take them as they are, then proceed to construct from them our picture of the world and of our place in it.

It is as a corollary of these indisputable facts about human life that we say that our attitude towards, reverence for, even our thought about other persons as well as the objects with which we are surrounded and the society of men in which we play our part, will be determined in large measure, if (as is clearly the case) not entirely, by the way we act towards them, the *physical* attitudes we take and the *bodily* movements we make. It is not for nothing, to take the most obvious example, that physical intercourse is an essential part of marriage. The union of bodies there achieved is indispensable for the realization of the state of love between man and woman. A marriage which is not consummated is a truncated marriage; a human love which does not have such normal physical expression is less than it should be.

Even in friendships something of the same sort holds true. An acquaintance of the writer's who is notoriously lax in responding to or himself writing letters (and in this way maintaining what, in effect, is a material means of contact with his acquaintances) once remarked that he felt friendship did not depend at all on continued relationships sustained by such "materialistic means." Of course, the result of his attitude was that his friendships tended to fade and become matters of "far away and long ago." We cannot hope to sustain our human relationships without some expression which brings us together with our friends and acquaintances. A friendship may be as "spiritual" as you please, but it must be continued, if it is to be continued at all, in the terms of the meetings in which the eye sees, the ear hears, the hand shakes another hand, as well as in terms of "the meeting of true minds."

Nor is it dissimilar in our more general relations with others. It is a widely accepted fact that "manners maketh man," to use William of Wykeham's famous phrase. The lifting of the hat, the waving of the hand, the little courtesies of life, the standing when an older person comes into a room, the polite action of holding chairs for women, bowing or nodding—all of these things, which to many seem quite trivial and unimportant, have their real and highly significant place not only in the ordered round of social intercourse but in the cultivation of friendly, courteous, decent states of mind and ways of adjustment to our fellowmen. It is likewise instinctive, as we say, for men to use these actions to express their atitudes and ways of thinking. Their fashions, their manners, their *mores* in the wider sense may vary from place to place and time to time, but the fact of expression is still a real and utterly essential fact.

Towards objects as well as towards persons this is also a necessity. The lover with the picture of his beloved or with some treasured gift from her, the soldier or patriotic citizen treating the flag or emblem with respect, even the child with its dolls . . . these are in line with that principle which we have laid down—that bodily action both expresses and develops the mental life. If we should endeavor to eradicate all such from our behavior pattern, we should not only be greatly impoverished beings; we should indeed cease to be genuinely human beings.

A good illustration of the point which we have been making is some ceremony such as a presidential inauguration in which all sorts of external actions are employed to manifest and impress inner states. The Bible upon which an oath is taken, the flags which are draped about the scene, the music which is played, the salutes, the crowd which stands when the Chief Executive enters the place of meeting— here are some among the hundreds of bits of materiality which are essential to the reality. Even the dress which is worn, uniforms and formal attire of one sort or another, has its part. On an entirely different level, a college fraternity initiation may also be used to illustrate the point. There, underneath the frivolity and seriousness of the *externalia*, something is believed to be accomplished. Lasting impressions are made and ways of behaving confirm the mental state which is the inner reality of the exercise.

Our discussion has been on the level of the secular. But it is necessary to approach our subject from this point of view, for as we have said above, it is important to understand the truth about man as man before we go on to discuss the truth of man as

a religious being.   It is in the religious field with
which in this essay we are more directly concerned
that there is a tendency to forget man's natural "en-
mannedness," which means body as well as soul, the
material as well as the spiritual, the means of expression as well as that which is to be expressed.   A
truer and deeper understanding of man himself may
help to prevent us from falling into the error of attempting to treat man the religious being as if he
were not really man at all, but a pale and disem-
bodied creature, lacking that richness and warmth
which is so genuine and lovely if often so dangerous
a thing—the fact that we live not so much *in* bodies
but *as* bodies in a world of bodies—human or social,
organic or inorganic.   *We* (*i.e.*, our innermost self,
our rational soul) live *as* body (*i.e.*, dependent upon,
expressed through, and living by means of dust and
dirt, actions and gestures, things done and things
said).   It is a strange thing, perhaps, that this
should be so, but it is the fact; and facts are here to
be accepted and transformed, not to be refused, denied or neglected.

3. THE WORLD OF SPIRIT AND OF SENSE

Two classical and sharply opposing positions have been taken concerning the nature of the vast world in which our little human life is set. One of these is the strictly naturalistic position—often enough, this becomes, reductively, a sheer materialism. For those who hold this view, the world in its entirety is non-spiritual; it is nothing but matter-in-motion. For the supporter of the other position, the world is entirely spiritual, and the problem is to explain why anyone has ever thought that there was such a thing as "matter." For those who hold this position, "all is mind," "spirit is everything." Here are two entirely contradictory ways of viewing the world.

Now it is apparent to anyone—or it ought to be apparent—that there is much to be said for each one of these notions. So far as the former or naturalistic view is concerned, there can be little doubt that observation of the world, whether it be the naïve realistic apprehension of it which necessarily marks the ordinary man in living his daily life or whether it be the sophisticated approach with precise instruments such as is found amongst the scientifically minded, does seem to tell us that that world is a material affair. Surely we never *see* or *hear* or *touch*, in any literal sense, that which is called "spiritual." In consequence, it might be contended and indeed has often been believed that anything by way of value or ideal, spirit or soul, even purpose or intention, if not entirely non-existent and illusory, is at least in character "epiphenomenal" (to use once again the word coined, it seems, by W. K. Clifford).

These non-material things, while they may be there, are then taken to be nothing more than ineffectual by-products or appearances; in terms of the illustration used in the preceding chapter, they are like the steam which pours from the locomotive —it is certainly present, but it is not the driving power of the engine.

The crass man or woman of affairs, whose creed is that "business is business," is likely much of the time to hold to some such sheer "common-sense" view, as he would inaccurately call it. And many scientists of the day-before-yesterday, if not the scientists of today, were quite ready, even anxious, to agree with them. What was the real stuff of the world? Sometimes it was hard atoms, whirling fortuitously through the space-time continuum; sometimes it was highly refined electrical particles or waves of energy. In any case, it was substance of a material sort . . . and there was nothing more. Or, if there were something more, it did not really *do* anything. Since Professor Whitehead and many others have come on the scientific scene and have taken to writing about the metaphysical bases of science, things are a little different, even in strictly scientific circles. In fact, it might be said that science in our own day and in the persons of some of its eminent expounders is in danger of shifting over to the opposite view—that all is spirit and that the material world is in reality nothing but the shadow of "mind." So say or hint some of our philosophically minded scientific writers, like Sir James Jeans and the late Sir Arthur Eddington.

While the crass naturalism which we have sketched may seem to many to be quite certainly the obvious truth, there is always (as William James, ever apt to say things both brilliantly and incisively, put it) a spirit in man which when he has come to such a sheer naturalistic conclusion whispers "Bosh!" The world is not really, even to naive experience, what we see when a naturalist in the reductive sense paints the picture. It is very different indeed.

Nor, on the other hand, is it like the picture given us by the sheer spiritualist. There are some people who think that they live in a world which is entirely mind or spirit, and in which there is nothing at all remotely resembling matter or stuff or physical energy or material objects. Certain of these folk would talk about the *appearances* of matter, which they would seek to explain away either as illusion or as error. In point of fact, however, even the most spiritual of us is forced to live *as if* there were a material world. We must eat food, which is a physical thing; we must wear clothing, which is made of material stuff; we must meet and have business relations with other persons, who seem to be fairly tangible realities; we must travel on trains, dwell in houses, dig gardens, mine ore and tap fuel; we are obliged to take what is on this reading only "illusion and error" so very seriously that it seems likely that the "spiritualist" himself, unless he has taken leave of his mind, must have a doubt now and again of the truth of his professed creed. Perhaps the spirit within him also whispers "Bosh!"

There are certain thinkers who talk as if "values" were the only genuine existents. These platonically-inclined folk, who have much to say about "ideals" and "values," will declare that "goodness, truth and beauty" are all that matter; indeed, they will say that these are all that genuinely exists. Sometimes these people write beautifully about their concern for such high or supreme values; occasionally, they try to live by them and to disregard the material world entirely, or (as they would say if they fell back into the idiom of the typical "spiritualist"), they intend to live in terms of reality and not in terms of appearances. In his more recent books Aldous Huxley has spoken in this fashion. Perhaps it is significant that he entitled one of them *Eyeless in Gaza;* it certainly seems as if he had shut his natural eyes, or even gouged them out, so that he could contemplate spiritual reality with his mind's eye alone and without being greatly concerned about such deliverances from the outside world as his natural vision might have given him. Even in scientific circles, as we have just indicated, there has been a sort of return to "spiritualism"—and in some sections of their prolific literary output, as we hinted, Sir James Jeans and Sir Arthur Eddington have appeared to deny that there is any *real* world beyond the world of mind or apart from that world.

Once again and in point of fact, however, how is it that we come to know of values? Surely, both common-sense and our ordinary experience will tell us, if we attend to them, that it is in, through, with and under the materiality of the world. There can be little serious doubt that for the normal business of daily living we accept the world as being composed largely of *stuff,* no matter how complex it may be or how knotted up it may have become in various concrete objects, from protons and neutrons up to lovely human forms and faces. Neither can there be any serious doubt that we are not content normally and naturally to leave it there. Rather, it is our experience that from the given and experienced materiality of things we go on to find spiritual realities, purposes, values and ideals which are somehow me-

diated to us in and through these "materialities."
Furthermore, so far as our ordinary living is concerned, we tend surely to take for granted that whatever may be the reality or power upon which the
world itself finally depends for its existence, that reality is disclosed to us not *in spite of* but *through*
and *by means of* the material and physical world.
On this point we shall speak at greater length in
our next chapter; yet our present discussion would
be seriously incomplete if we did not at least mention it here.

Let us consider some of the "supreme values"—
specifically the three—goodness, truth and beauty—
which are often called the "Platonic triad." How
did we ever come to know of the idea, not to say the
ideal, of beauty? It is surely a fact that no man has
looked upon Beauty, plain and unmeditated. When
we talk as if a man had done so—and admittedly we
often do speak in this way—we are simply employing
a kind of short-hand speech for the more accurate
statement that when brought face to face with certain harmonious configurations, either of sound or of
color or of line, men have been conscious of a reality
which they find or conceive to be somehow present
in all harmony and which they have called "Beauty."
We are not concerned to press even our own way of
expressing this. It is not necessary to accept any
special theory of the nature of aesthetic experience,
nor to hold to any particular set of ideas concerning
"ideal forms," in order to recognize the fact that
sheer beauty in itself is not known to us. We know
and see and admire beautiful objects, whether in
nature or in the world of art; we create these objects, somehow tracing in material things the harmony which is spoken to our minds . . . but there is
no beauty without mediation, and therefore beauty

comes to be adjectival although none the less real. It is adjectival in that it is a qualification of and involves a relationship to some object or scene or melody; it is real, in that it is not simply a way in which *we* look at the object or scene or melody, but is inherent in the thing itself, recognized and appreciated by the observer or the hearer.

The situation in regard to goodness is exactly parallel. It is not possible for us to look upon the sheer unmediated Good. What in truth we do see and know is goodness embodied in persons or things. If we mean ethical goodness, we find it only in good persons or good deeds. If it is goodness in the sense of the infinitely desirable, or even in the sense merely of the desirable as such, it too is embodied for us in other human beings or in material things. A good painting, a good friendship, a good meal—here are embodiments, varying greatly in their degree of desirability, of that which is desirable to us, attractive to us, good. Even if we happened to be Kantians in the realm of ethics, and so held firmly to the categorical imperative as the key to moral conduct, we should yet be obliged to admit that we had never seen, nor could we quite understand how we might ever see, the sheer *oughtness* in things, or the sheer sense of obligation in persons. What we do know is that there are persons whose behavior reflects, more or less adequately, the devotion to duty which Kant commends; there are objects which, we say, are more or less satisfactory in approximating the "whatever it is" that they ought to be.

Even in the matter of truth—third in the list of "values" which we have called the "Platonic triad" —it must be said that we are dealing, in our human experience, only with embodiment. It requires little proof to recognize that the world does not give us,

direct and unmediated, *the* Truth. What we have in
our ordinary business of living is mediated truth—
statements which are said to be true; accuracies
which are believed to be discoverable; near corres-
pondences with "that which is" which are taken for
very close representations of the "facts." The most
adequate scientific equation is not the truth; it is, at
best, a truthful equation, corresponding so far as
may be to certain conditions and stating so far as
may be certain discoverable relationships or factual
data. And in philosophy, it would be a brave thinker
who claimed that he had actually got in his hands,
so to say, and then put down on paper, not alone a
certain amount of truthful statement but (in the
genuine meaning of the term) "the Truth." Perhaps the closest approach to such a claim is made
by Hegel, with his identification of rationality and
reality. Yet we may be allowed to guess that it is
hardly likely that Hegel himself, in his more modest
moments, really wished to imply that he had done
other than give what unquestionably he considered
the finally accurate *statement* of things. But even
for Hegel that would not *in itself* have been Truth,
sheer and unadulterated.

This, however, is only one side of the matter. It
is apparent that we come to know values and purposes in terms of materiality. Even when we wish
to speak of the meaning of the world or the intention which operates it, we are obliged to recognize
these as declared to us in what happens and what
can be observed as happening. But it is also true that
it is only possible for values, purposes, meanings,
spiritual realities and ideals of any sort, to "get
across" to us in precisely such terms and through
such material means of expression. Much of this we
have already understood as given fact when we con-

sidered the nature of man himself. There is need to make the point there. But it is also true of the world at large . . . if value is to be realized, it is fairly obvious that it must be realized *in* something; if there is goodness to be expressed, it must be expressed somewhere, in some place, through some object; if beauty is to manifest itself, it must employ some particular configurations for its statement. The world seems to be built this way. Perhaps it may be offensive to our sense of decency that such is the way in which it is built, but it will not do much good to quarrel with things that are inevitable.

A further extension of the position which we have been enunciating in the preceding paragraphs is the recognition that the world is not only so constituted on its natural and physical side, but also so far as the order of society is concerned. The truth is that social conveyance of value is in the same case as the general "embodiment-principle" in the natural world would indicate operates for sheer physical realities. Not only in the world of our physical experience, but also in that of our social experience, there can be little doubt that so-called moral, spiritual and aesthetic values are conveyed through media which in this instance are of a social nature. Traditions of art and of moral custom will illustrate the point. Not even the most individualistic of us can cut himself loose from his "social conditioning"; we are dependent for our values, even for our values when we contradict them, upon that appurtenance to a social tradition which is ours by reason of the fact that we are men and by that token members of the human race and of human social groups.

Furthermore, the values, be they aesthetic or ethical or patriotic or in any other category, require for their continuance among us, as well as for their conveyance to us, social groups of various kinds. Without these, they would die off or fade away; by these, they are made living realities in the continuing experience of men. We should not even know of some of our most highly prized truths were it not for the fact that somebody in the past had stated them, a social group had remembered them, and the corporate human "memory" had retained them and handed them down to us—through books, perhaps. Paintings have to be done on canvas. Ideas, attitudes, ways of thinking and behaving, require some verbal or other embodiment or some statement in material terms which shall make them capable of enduring in a world that is in its given nature a strange compound of spirit and sense, of fact and value, of purpose and material stuff.

Baron Friedrich von Hügel has argued this point at length, in his invaluable discussion of the place of institutions in man's life in *Essays and Addresses*. It is not only in the strictly moral realm that such institutional embodiment is found; it is found in this *and* in every other range of life, not excluding the scientific. There is a scientific tradition; there are societies, such as the Royal Society in England or the American Association for the Advancement of Science in this country, which are the agencies through which the great scientific tradition is both preserved and conveyed. Even if by some action of a perverse dictator these and similar organized groups should be entirely abolished, there would still be the carrying on of the tradition through written material, through records of experiments, through specimens which were safeguarded for future generations to study. In the realm of national affairs, likewise, social tradition is to be found ... the flag, the Constitution, the Bill of Rights, the letters, speeches and papers of the "founding fathers," are all of them means by which what has been called "the American spirit" is expressed and known. Patriotic fervor itself is aroused when the citizen is brought to realize that he is one of a group, historically continuous with the long past of the group, dedicated to the same ideals and ideas, loyal to the same purpose and principles.

Now this experience of men in the various areas of their life is inevitably expressed in rites and ceremonies of one sort or another. Precisely as man requires physical media to know and understand the truths about his world; precisely as he requires sensible means of expressing his own innermost self— so he requires for expression of social attitudes and allegiances, for expression of adherence to standards and ideas, some definite and even prescribed ways in which he shall both state and at the same time make more vivid to himself the particular notion or attitude or emotion which he has at heart. The saluting of the flag, the public taking of an oath, the ceremonies of Memorial Day and Independence Day, are all of them illustrations of this truth. The natural solidarity of men is expressed and enhanced in their fraternal organizations—that is why lodges and clubs and societies for promoting "causes" have come into existence. And once men have "got together," there are rites and ceremonies which are part of the "togetherness," with actions and gestures and words and sensible signs of various kinds that are intrinsic elements in the whole transaction. Here we are face to face with a given fact about human nature, about society, and about the world in which both are placed.

Man is, then, a being who is largely active in terms of "response." The world in its physical as-

pect, conveying to him the spiritual realities which
are in and behind it, and similarly the world in its
sociological aspect, making real to him ethical and
countless other values, presses in upon this human
organism, "getting at him" (so to say) through sensible media—the five senses and all the other means
of impression which are part of the human body.
By these means he is stirred to action, moved to
thought, driven to conclusions. It is true, as we
carefully pointed out in the last chapter, that man
is an *initiating* agent; but it would appear that his
capacity for initiation is itself initially dependent
upon the prior impact of reality upon him. No ideas
can, as it were, originate in him *entirely* independent-
ly of the outside world. His genuine originality and
his genuine initiating activity are, as it were, first
the *arranging of* and then the *acting upon* that
which reaches him through sensible means. Once
the process has been inaugurated, there is then a
continuous give-and-take, and the actions which are
performed on man's part do in fact not only express
the attitudes, ideas and emotions which are his own,
but they also modify and profoundly change the
world itself which lies beyond his own "spiritual"
reach.

Man, we have seen, is not confined to his body as
if it were (in the ancient Pythagorean dictum) "the
prison house of his soul." Rather the body is the
wonderfully adjusted and amazingly delicate instrument by which man acts and by which also the world
makes itself known to the man who acts. Furthermore, as we have argued in the present chapter, the
very world itself and human society as a whole when
interpreted in the light of the common-sense outlook
of the ordinary man, are also in a wonderful way
the union of two factors, factors which may be called

in each one of these instances (as also in man himself) *body* or sense, and *spirit* or mind. Here it is, then: spirit and sense, a dualism which is not merely a parallelism, but one in which spirit acts upon sense, sense acts upon spirit.

Professor J. B. Pratt, years ago, took his stand for such a view in a valuable and perhaps forgotten little book called *Matter and Spirit*. With whatever qualifications recent discoveries may have necessitated, his position seems vindicated by the sheer facts of ordinary experience. Likewise the great American philosopher, William James, in his two-volume work on psychology, contended for the facts of bodily action *and* mental action. James was intent upon insisting that we recognize the full reality of both these sides of man, but he also made it clear that the expression-impression factor in man is dependent upon his bodily nature, in its widest as well as in its most precise sense. And in more recent times, Dr. William Temple in *Nature Man and God*, Professor A. E. Taylor in *The Faith of a Moralist*, and (before either of these books was written) Baron von Hügel in his *Eternal Life, Essays and Addresses*, and posthumously in *The Reality of God*, have taken their stand with common-sense and ordinary human experience. It might be said that both sheer materialism or naturalism, and sheer spiritualism or mentalism, have had their day; and it is remarkable that from the scientific side, a thinker of the stature of Professor Whitehead has come to the same view as that which the philosophers whom we have mentioned have found to be the only adequate one. Mr. Whitehead is particularly useful to our discussion because of his insistence on that interpretation of reality which holds that the element of value is intrinsic to fact. By implication, he is impelled to the recognition of the true relationship between the two —ideal, spiritual, mental "data" as mediated by, but yet supervenient to, the factual, physical, material realm.

With such testimony from such experts, confirming the deliverances of common-sense and the ordinary experience of ordinary men in their day-by-day living, it may not unfairly be concluded that the field is open for such a view of the world as we have indicated: neither sheer materialism nor sheer spiritualism, but "incarnationalism,"—an "incarnational world," in which matter is used by spirit and spirit is disclosed through matter, each operating in and with the other.

There is one important safeguard which we should wish to add. The realm of mind or spirit, whose *hither* aspect we discern in these operations, stretches off into unexplored and unexplorable remoteness at its farther side, thus preserving in our human experience that "attitude of tip-toe expectancy," as von Hügel called it, which depends upon the felt presence of the "more" that subsists *beyond* the known and the knowable, a "more" ready to break in upon us with fuller and richer meaning, but yet a "more" which is never exhaustible by the human mind, the mind which works through sensible agencies to come into union with the world that is not itself.

This element of the "more"—or, philosophically expressed, the transcendent—has been particularly stressed for us by the poets of our race. The constant recognition of the "more" that lies "beyond" our experience is the explanation of that insistence that "every bush is aflame," as Mrs. Browning said; of that perception that "the sunset touch, the fancy from a flower-bell . . ." and the rest (of which her husband wrote) can speak meaning deeper than ordinary or even poetic description can put into words; of that longing, expressed by a much greater poet, for "the farther shore," because there are *lachrimae rerum;* for that insight found universally in men who at some point in their lives have been touched by the world of spirit as it spoke expressively and evocatively to them through the humdrum events of daily experience, or called to them in some high moment when a casual contact became the conveyer of a depth of significance such as no feeble human words could ever adequately state.

Such is our world — a world of meanings, of values, of spiritual significances, of purpose, of mind; but a world in which these are given to us and known by us under signs, through sacraments and by means of symbols. It is a world, furthermore, in which there is a social handing-on of these meanings, values, spiritual significances, of this purpose and of this mind, through institutional embodiments or social groups each with its own distinctive and particular rites and ceremonies, actions and phrases, gestures and formulae. Finally, it is a world in which, so far as we can see, man (constituted as he is with an indispensable sensible medium for his apprehension) could not and would not know of the meanings, values and spiritual significances, nor of mind and purpose, were these not brought to him in an embodied form. And this is the meaning of the term "incarnational," in its very widest sense.

It is natural, therefore, that in the realm of the religious, men should have behaved in a fashion which involved the use of the body and all that speaks to it and for it. And it is extraordinary to notice the unnatural fashion in which otherwise discerning thinkers have endeavored to treat this one

area of life as if it could be entirely separated from
all the rest.   There are those who have written as if
in this one area, separated in this unnatural fashion
from all the rest, there could be ways of behaving
which are utterly incongruous both to the world and
also to man himself.   Of course, in point of fact,
the separation is never really effected.   Even in the
most rigidly puritanical and anti-incarnational religions, there is inevitably *some* bodily expression,
even if it be merely verbal.   There is always *some*
natural means employed, even if it be merely a book
in which words are written or a building in which
worship is offered.   And there is necessarily some
embodiment of the object or value or being towards
which religion is the human movement, even if it be
only a form of words (for then it must be a mental
concept which has its physical side) ; or (as is more
often the case) some energy or power disclosed in
the whole range of things but never condescending
to the particularity of place and time (for even so
it is the physical reality of "the light of setting suns"
which speaks, to the devotee, of the existence or
character of that power).

In our next chapter we shall turn to a consideration of the nature of man as the religious animal,
his ways of behaving and his modes of adaptation to
that which he calls "the divine" or his "god."   We
shall then be ready to proceed to a study of the specifically Christian facts and ideas that have a bear-
ing upon the sign-sacrament-symbol complex.   At
the moment we have arrived at the point where we
can say with assurance that not only is man himself
an "incarnational" being, composed of mind and
body, but that the world and human society as a
whole are in the same category, for in each of them
that which is spiritual is present through and conveyed by that which is material and physical.

4. MAN AS THE RELIGIOUS ANIMAL

Many attempts have been made to single out the particular characteristic which marks man out as *man*, different from the other animals who inhabit this globe. The results of such a study have been various, as various indeed as the particular prejudices with which the investigators have begun their work. One attempt has been successful, however, in that it was concerned merely to describe the facts about man and his behavior, such as are discernible to anyone who endeavors objectively to look at the picture. This has resulted in the *dictum* that man, while he is an animal, is an animal of "a rational nature." That is, he is an animal who thinks, who varies in his responsive adjustment to the world according to his own "ideas," and who can to some degree determine his conduct according to "rational" principles. The scholastic definition of man, therefore, as "an animal with a rational nature," is not so much a definition as a description from observation; and it includes within it the wisdom of prior observation and thought which had come to some such understanding of man's uniqueness although it had not stated it in precisely these words.

To say that man has, or is, a rational nature is to say, in Augustinian language, that he possesses memory, will and understanding. We do not imply that these three *equal* the rationality of man; rather they are modes in which man's rationality *operates*. In any case, however, man is a being who can remember the past, and in the light of that past can make adjustments to the present and prepare for the future. He can determine on operations and activities, and pour energy into them. And he can recognize, describe, and grasp the meaning of things as they are presented to him, or as he orders and arranges them according to patterns which seem to him to spring from or to be necessary for comprehending that which is apprehended by him.

Now all of this is true. But there is another important fact about man, which while it may not be the singularly differentiating fact, philosophically speaking, is yet a very important fact, and one which observation will at once suggest. This is that man is the animal who is *religious*. This strange biped, living on a planet over which he has won a large measure of control but upon which he still remains utterly dependent for physical life and sustenance, seeks constantly to relate himself to some stretch of reality which is beyond the purely mundane. Baron von Hügel, in his striking study entitled *The German Soul,* has said that it is man's uneasiness in the world, the sense of a vastness which is beyond him, his idealism and his despair, which points towards the truth that man, in the profound recesses of his being and sometimes almost unknown to his conscious mind, recognizes or senses, in some degree and fashion, that there is some range of being, some real object, some supernatural realm, with which he *ought* to be in touch, and with which he *does* feel himself to be in touch now and again at the higher and more illuminating as well as the deeper and more penetrating moments of his experience. From the wildest savage to the most highly sophisticated man of letters, this phenomenon is to be found. Even when it is denied its specifically or normal religious form of expression, it yet persists under some

strange and often very surprising *incognito*. Man
is incurably religious, although he may not be religious in any of the conventional and usual ways.

What then, is religion? Here again there have
been innumerable suggestions as to definition, rang-
ing all the way from the sense of comradeship with
"the friend behind phenomena" to the sheer self-
abnegation of the fanatical devotee. And here also
we are not obliged to single out any one of the countless possible definitions as being exclusively true.
In fact, it is likely that there is value and sense in
all of the suggested descriptions of the nature of religion. Each of them, doubtless, has meanings, if
not for every man, at least for some men as they experience life in its richness and fullness. Yet it may
be said that the sort of experience suggested, on the
one hand, by Schleiermacher, and on the other, by
Baron von Hügel, will come fairly close to being the
most common characteristic in religion. In the German religious philosopher, the central point of religion is some consciousness, on the part of the experiencing person, of dependence on a *something*
which may be defined in various ways. In the Scot-
tish-German theologian-philosopher, it is "sheer
adoration." These two ideas, which seem to be different ways of stating the same kind of attitude,
should be taken in combination with the view of
Rudolf Otto. Otto maintains that the sense of the
"holy," the compelling yet demanding "other," the
"numinous," is the differentiating quality in *religious*
dependence or *religious* adoration as distinct from
any other "dependence" or "adoration." In these
views, seen synthetically, we should say that we have
come to an inclusive and suggestive statement that
is at least adequate for our purposes.

In Schleiermacher, the stress is laid on the sense

or feeling that one has no existence as and of oneself, that one is held in being by something else, and
that one must be related to that something as a dependent being who recognizes and accepts the fact
of his dependence. In von Hügel, the stress is on the
active acceptance, manifested in intentional and
grateful self-giving, of the fact of one's dependence
—one bows down and adores the transcendent Other
upon which one depends. And in Otto, there is the
recognition, which is sufficiently clear and admirably
stated in von Hügel although not so clear if in fact
really present at all in Schleiermacher, that the *That*
on which one is dependent and which one adores is
altogether "holy," separated out from the rest of the
world even if present in it, claiming utter and willing
obedience and demanding the free response of worship. In this central sense or feeling which marks
the religious man, there are always present the two
elements, first of overwhelming attraction towards
the religious object, which draws the worshiper as a
magnet, and then the awe or reverence which requires him to approach cautiously, to hold back for
fear of trespass on "holy ground," to cover his eyes
lest he be blinded by the "splendor of light."

It is our conviction that something like this total
and complete attitude is the most widespread of religious experiences, from primitive man to cultured
man. Obviously it will be found to vary in intensity,
not unlike a sense of music or the gift for ethical
discernment; but it is a constant factor in man's on-
going life—and while we cannot claim that it is *all*
there is to religion, we can certainly insist that without it, religion would not be what historically and
observably it has been.

Granted, then, that religion is (or at least centrally involves) something like this, let us proceed

to consider the ways in which this "religiosity" of man has expressed itself. If we have approached anywhere near the truth in our analysis of the nature of man and his relation to the world about him, in the discussion in earlier chapters, we should expect to find that man takes, in religion, a material way of expression. And it is clear enough that this is what we do indeed find. Anthropological investigations make it plain to us that a sheerly "spiritual" religion is unknown to the human race, at least so far as these investigations have gone up to the present. Man's materiality governs his religious life, as it governs all the rest of his experience.

Nor is this all. Man, as religious animal, believes that the religious object, whatever it may be, *acts* upon him. It is, indeed, not so much *object* in the first instance as *subject*. And it acts upon him, not through unmediated spiritual means, but precisely through material realities. Not only does primitive man seem universally to believe this, but the most highly developed religious instinct, as manifested in the prophetic tradition of the Hebrew religion, illustrates the same general principle. The prophets received their messages, for the most part, through visions or auditions which were interpreted to them by the Lord God but which as *visions* or *auditions* were the means by which the specific religious truth, with which they were to be entrusted, was conveyed. In addition, the vindication of their prophecy was always in some action, which was believed to be divinely controlled—as, for example, the moving down of the Assyrians on the little Jewish nation, as vindicating by a divinely governed act, on a material plane, the vision of the prophet Amos who had seen the divine reality expressed to him in physical form —the plumb-line, the basket of summer fruit, etc.

Even amongst the Hindus, a people prone perhaps more than any other to a non-material kind of
speculation so far as their philosophical theology has
been concerned, we note that the need for accommo-
dation to the ordinary requirements of human experience has demanded that there should be *avatars*,
or human and sometimes other material embodiments (even if these be docetic, or phantomlike, embodiments) of the truths which are otherwise taught
by the sages. "Truth embodied in a tale" has entered in where "truth in closest words" or in most
ultra-spiritual concepts could not make any entrance.

Let us take, as an example of primitive religion,
worship centered about some natural object—say, a
stone believed to be "holy." The "holy" stone which
is believed to be the dwelling-place of the divine has
frequently been grievously misunderstood by some
western students of religion. It is not at all a merely superstitious object. It is, on the contrary, a
place where according to the savage's belief the divine power or energy is released and becomes operative upon human creatures, or where that power is
present to invigorate them. The stone must therefore be approached with awe, with reverence, yet
with great desire and interest, because it is the spot
where *That* upon which the worshiper is dependent
makes itself known and available to him. Some of
those who have made a special study of the matter,
from the side of scientific anthropology, may and indeed do differ from our conclusion at this point.
Yet it is our opinion that provided the study is scientific *and* sympathetic, and not governed by the prejudices of our own age or theory, the best reconstruc-
tion of the results of investigation will be to see that
the materiality of the *object*—to use this name for
any and every physical, tangible, visible, reality in

primitive religion—is both *essential* to the transaction between the divine "something" and the worshiper, and also is not in itself, as physical, the *whole end* or goal of the transaction. In other words, the primitive heathen does not "bow down to wood and stone," even in his own limited and totally unsophisticated understanding of the matter; he bows down to some reality which speaks to him, acts upon him, is known to him *through* "wood and stone."

As we move higher in the scale of religious expression, we find that the element of materiality is not lost, but is developed and made more precise and significant in its operation in the divine-human relation. The Jewish race, while it gave up "images" and the worship of them (as it was called), did not entirely give up the use of material things in religious expression. The Ark, whatever its origin or nature, was the "dwelling-place" of Jahweh; the Temple at Jerusalem was the central scene of his worship and the "place where his honor dwelt." Even when the inner-life of man—his "soul" or whatever other word happened to be used to describe this principle—came to be seen as the unique earthly tabernacle or dwelling-place of God, it was none the less a material reality, namely the body of man, which was the means of expression for that "inner God." The element of materiality was not lost; what happened was that its *point and significance* were made both wider and deeper.

It is obvious that in the highest expressions of historic Christian devotion, the same is true. To this we shall turn for more detailed examination in our next chapter. But at the moment we would emphasize the fact that the whole range of man's religious life (Christian and other) goes to show the inter-relationship of spirit and sense. Not only is

the divine object worshiped and made known (by
his prevenient action) through material things or
actions; the worshiper himself invariably uses such
things or actions for his adoration. He indulges in
bodily acts, often strange and (to us) barbaric. He
makes material offerings, sometimes of a crude and
horrible sort, such as human-sacrifice. He engages
in ritual-ceremonial expressions, including the dance,
music, and all the wide variety of apparatus in primitive, developing and sophisticated worship.

Nor is this merely to express, from his side out-
wards, so to say, his religious impulses. There is
the reverse operation—the bodily acts, material objects, *etc.*, are used to impress upon himself the
sense of awe, of communion, of sacrifice, of love.
von Hügel has remarked upon this in another connection; "The bridge between sense and spirit (is)
demonstrably intended for traffic in both directions"
(*German Soul*, p. 170). Religious man illustrates
this truth, when (for example) a Christian takes the
Crucifix (as von Hügel goes on to say) not only "as
expressing faith" but also as to be "used to awaken
faith." In non-Christian religious systems—so
widely different as Hinduism with its lustrations, for
instance; Mohammedanism with its turning to the
East and its ordained prostrations in worship of
Allah; and the strange ceremonial self-mutilations
of certain African tribes—there is always this "two-
way traffic" between spirit and sense. The religious
action, in all its materiality, is certainly an expression from within or a way of stating an interior
mood or feeling. It is also, and perhaps more deeply,
recognized as valuable and therefore employed because it awakens and strengthens a specific religious
emotion and a specific religious conviction . . . *and
also*, because it is the way in which, so it is believed,

the divine in itself is "got across," or better (since the divine is subject in the first instance) "gets itself across," to the worshiper.

The *social* aspect of man's religion is also to be emphasized as an essential and intrinsic element in the total picture. Mr. Whitehead has urged us to take religion as being fundamentally "what a man does with his solitariness." This has truth in it and, we may add, a very important truth; but it overlooks the fact that man's religion as actually operative in human history and discovered by scientific anthropology is found in social forms. Even in the most exclusively spiritual types of religion among Christians, such as that seen in the Society of Friends, there are social forms. It may be contended, therefore, that there is considerable truth in Durkheim's notion that religion and sociality are closely linked, although it is apparent that his simple identification of the two is a serious fallacy. This view of Durkheim's is considered at some length in another essay in the present volume.

When we consider the historical development of man as a religious animal, we are more and more impressed by the fact that religion invariably comes to him as in some sense a *tradition*. That is to say, it is something which is "handed down" from the past and "handed over" from his social group. Frequently that ends the story—the religion is simply accepted as *given*, and then either taken with the sheerest conventionality or used with the deepest devotion; in both cases, the result is what Bergson has called a "closed" system of religious life. When, on the other hand, some great creative leader emerges and an "opening" is made in the "closed" system, so that a new inrush of life may be possible and new developments may occur, it is still in some social

form that the religion with its new insight or belief
goes on and grows. When the prophet feels that he
must break with established ideas, it is still ordinar-
ily his feeling that "I and the little band that thou
hast given me" (to use one of Isaiah's sayings as an
illustration) will either preserve the old truth or will
move out into new truth when the settled established
community no longer has any interest in one or the
other. The "come-outers," as they were called in
New England, may have "come out" one by one, but
they soon formed groups of "come-outing" believers
and found for their new religious life a social means
of expression.

In the higher and highest religions known to us,
this social transference and traditional mediation of
belief at length reaches the level of specifically religious *communities* or "churches." But farther
down, where such definite groupings are not to be
discovered, the transference and mediation of religious conviction and religious experience is none the
less through accepted social and traditional forms or
through community-influences which are almost unconsciously absorbed, often indeed without any conscious effort, in childhood and through tribal contacts or national and racial fellowship. The ideas
which are always implicitly involved in and sometimes clearly expressed through tribal ceremonial
are dependent upon some specifically social action in
order to reach into and affect the participant. And
when the great leaps in religious insight have occurred—frequently they have been *very* great—they
have not taken people away from their group, in the
long run; or, if they have done so, they have brought
them into another and (it has been thought) more
significant and valuable group to which they must
belong. In truth, it may be said that the most

marked dissenters are often those who are most dependent upon the community or tradition which they deplore and from which they take their departure. The phrase, "take their departure" may be used in two senses, as we all know. Often enough in religious history the two senses are in fact one sense—those who leave the fold usually have taken the fold along with them, although they may have done considerable re-interpretation and re-arrangement of that from which they have felt called to differ, and although they certainly may have added profoundly important and very considerable new elements to the original. And the fact that these new elements (given time and in the long run) may well modify seriously and perhaps alter radically the total resultant picture, does not negate the *original* dependence to which we referred.

Hence, while we insist upon the essential sociality *of* religion, we are not prepared to deny the profound individualistic strain *in* religion. On the contrary, it is probably the fact that the reality of "individualism" in religion—the "soul and God" of St. Augustine, the "what a man does with his solitariness" of Whitehead, the "two luminously clear realities" of Newman, *etc.,*—is to be found precisely at the core of the sociality of religion. While the lower interpretation may be that the particular man *loses* himself in his social group, the higher interpretation is that he *finds* himself there. He does not lose his unique individual relationship to God so much as he loses the peculiarities which would make that relationship unbalanced and disproportionate.

Mr. Tawney has remarked upon the fact that the man who seeks God apart from his fellows frequently finds not God but the devil; and he goes on to say that the devil, so found, often bears an embarrassing resemblance to the man who has been seeking. This is a somewhat piquant way of pointing out that one of the important functions of sociality, of the community, or of the group, in religion, is to give due value to *all* the variety which is found in the innumerable instances of individual religious life, and to suggest that while the individual must inevitably have his own unique relationship to the divine he should neither deny other men's relationships, each man for himself, nor fail to profit by them for the greater enhancement of his own unique relationship to God. Nor should he insist at any point or time on the *total* truth of his own peculiar contact. In other words, the social embodiment of religion is the means to humility, and humility is itself a reflection of that sense of dependence which is at the very heart of the religious life.

It is exceedingly unfortunate that so much has been said and written which would suggest if it does not positively assert that any and every material and social expression of religion is perverse and false. Perhaps this emphasis has been due not only to a puritanical distrust of the senses, but also to a philosophical prejudice in favor of "pure concepts" and in opposition to "imaginal thinking." Cartesian thought and its historical consequences in the last three hundred years of our western philosophical tradition would perhaps lead to the conclusion that it is only in ideas, supposedly clear and distinct but at any rate always mental, that truth ever really rests. It may be that the renewed understanding of man's organic relationship to his world, in Pringle-Pattison's phrase, an understanding which has led in our own day to such "organismic" philosophical systems as Whitehead's, will do much to restore the balance. For it is not only true that we do, in sheer fact, "think on our pulses," as Keats put it; it is also true that for most of us, most of the time, our emotional life and our sensible experience are our clearest indication of the wider ranges of reality which often enough our strictly conceptual thought misses almost completely.

Nor does such an insistence necessitate the cheapening of reason itself. It means, rather, a widening of the meaning of our reasoning, so that it is not simply "logic-chopping" but becomes reasonable response to reality in a wider sense. "Life is bigger than logic." So we are often told, and while the statement is frequently made in an effort to discount the value of logic, it need not be taken in that sense at all. St. Thomas Aquinas was eminently the logical thinker; yet we may be sure that he would have agreed with that dictum about logic. Logic, sheer conceptual rationality in terms of ideas, is invaluable and necessary, so that our thought may be as clear and as precise as possible, for it is the nature of the thinker to desire to think as clearly and as precisely as he can. But the world about us is known through the sensible means with which we are naturally endowed. Upon that world, so known to us, our minds get to work, seeking to arrange and order and select and discriminate significances, ranges of meaning, the important and the peripheral, *etc.* But the appeal is always back to experience, for checking and re-checking. And this writer, for one, is confident that even St. Thomas, the great rationalist of the middle ages, would have agreed to this kind of empiricism!

In any case, religiously speaking, the average man—and the highly sophisticated man in his average moments—is dependent upon signs, symbols and sacraments, in one form or another. A personal ex-

perience may be used to illustrate the point. The
writer was traveling with a friend, an advertising
man and a non-believer. They were visiting some
of the rather "unrestrained" churches in French
Canada, where piety has expressed itself in crude
crucifixes with great splashes of paint to represent
blood and with very realistic portrayal of horrible
sufferings, and where the companion statues of the
saints are not "formalized" according to our taste,
to put it mildly. During the excursion, the writer
unhappily ventured to express his disdain for this
sort of pious pictorial exaggeration. To his surprise,
his non-believing friend broke out, "That's the
trouble with you spiritual snobs; you can, or think
you can, say what you believe in words, but most
people can't, and if you were honest you'd know that
you can't. You've *got* to think through images."

Doubtless this was extreme, but it was a well-
deserved rebuke and it caused the writer to stop and
consider. He was obliged in all honesty to admit
that it was certainly true that in most of his thinking, most of the time, *sensibilia* somehow got into the
thought so that images were in his mind and not
sheer concepts alone. This was true in ordinary
thought about ordinary things. It was true even
philosophically, for the very concepts employed had
often if not always a certain indefinable pictorial
quality. Certainly and most significantly it was true
religiously. Was this due to the fact that he had
been brought up in "Catholic" ways? Or was it a
condition of all religious thought? With this in
mind, he enquired of others, non-believing or rationalist, Protestant as well as Catholic; and he discovered in practically every instance, even in those who
were most definitely "spiritual" in religious action
and most thoroughly deprecated the wide use of out-

ward means of worship, that their religious ideas
were "imaginally" known. The Crucifix might be
discarded, but yet the Protestant sang, "When I survey the wondrous Cross." The images, doubtless
somewhat refined, were there.

And they had to be there. It was inevitable and
inescapable, because man's sense-experience is the
source of his thought-material, and his world is a
mind-matter complex. In religion, as everywhere
else, we cannot avoid the facts.

Hence it may be said, as we survey the whole
range of man's religious life from the primitive
savage to the believer of the present day, that St.
Thomas Aquinas has correctly stated the truth:
"Now the human mind, in order to be united to God,
needs to be guided by the sensible world, since the
invisible things of God are clearly seen, being understood by the things that are made, as the Apostle
says *(Romans 1:20)*. Wherefore in divine worship
it is necessary to make use of corporeal things, that
man's mind may be aroused thereby, as by signs, to
the spiritual acts by means of which he is united to
God." *(S. T. II. 81.7)*. Thus, while in religion the
soul of man adores God, recognizing gladly its dependence upon him who is holy, and while it is therefore imperative to recognize that this is the *essence*
of the matter, yet (because man is what he is and is
constituted as he is constituted in a world which is
as it is) it is equally imperative to see again with St.
Thomas that "since we are composed of a two-fold
nature, intellectual and sensible, we offer God a two-
fold adoration; namely, a spiritual adoration, con-
sisting in the internal devotion of the mind; and a
bodily adoration, which consists in an exterior humb-
ling of the body," for "we exhibit signs of humility
in our bodies in order to incite our affections to sub-

mit to God" as well as to "signify our weakness in comparison of God." *(S. T. II. 84.2)*.

Our discussion has already reached over into the realm of Christian faith, theology and worship. But this is because Christianity, however new it may be in its essential gospel, yet speaks to man as man, and to man as religious animal. There must therefore be some overlapping, unless we subscribe to the Barthian thesis of a complete and total difference between Christianity and all other religion—a position that seems to us theologically heretical, historically false, philosophically nonsensical, psychologically unsound and practically impossible.

5. THE CHRISTIAN EXPRESSION OF RELIGION

The central belief of the historical Christian Church has always been the faith that in the humanity of Jesus of Nazareth, God Almighty walked the ways of this world. Or, to put it in another way, Christianity (as Soloviev, the Russian philosopher, once said) is distinctively faith in the divinity of Christ. That is by way of asserting that the unmeasured Godhead both chose and was able to express himself to men in and through human nature. He accommodated himself to the conditions of humanity, in order that he might make himself known and available to men in terms which were understandable to them. In

the message to the maid, the human birth,
the lesson, and the young man crucified

we have both seen and heard, touched and handled "the Word of Life." Or, in the climatic words of the preface to the Fourth Gospel, "the Word was made flesh and dwelt amongst us . . ."

Now it is obvious that this assertion is entirely in line with the general situation in regard to man and the conception of the universe which we have been describing in earlier chapters in this book. And it is noteworthy that the main current of Christian theology has always understood man and the world as we have described them. It has never interpreted life in terms of an abstract spirituality.

One of the earliest controversies in the Christian Church arose over the popular philosophy called gnosticism, which had its reflection within the circle of Christian theology proper in those who were called the "docetics." The view proposed by these men was that, because of God's utter purity and holiness, it was inconceivable that he should be con-

61

taminated by any contact with the world of matter and dirt. They were obliged therefore to say that the material world was not God's creation; it was either an "appearance" only, or if not that then an entirely unimportant and indeed regrettable and dangerous element which had no relationship with the divine reality. When these thinkers came to treat of the person of Christ, they made his humanity into nothing more than a masquerade-phantasm, which had about it no fundamental reality at all. In other representatives of the docetic theory, Christ had never really used his humanity but had pretended to use it. In any case, it was shameful to dwell upon his body; his "spirit" was the important thing.

The writings of St. Ignatius of Antioch, with his insistence that Jesus was truly born, truly suffered and truly died; and the great tractates of St. Irenaeus, of Clement of Alexandria and Origen, of Tertullian and of many other early apologists, were largely directed at insisting on the genuine reality of Jesus' human nature and human life, and were written against those who were attempting to reduce these to mere appearance or to unimportant and soon-discarded clothing assumed simply for the moment but never integral to the God in Jesus. The Church won its victory over gnosticism and the various docetic heresies only after long struggle and bitter controversy. But the Church had seen correctly how fundamental was the maintenance of the genuine reality of human nature in Jesus. It had understood that if this reality were denied, God in Jesus could and probably would become a phantom, too. It was precisely in the humanity, with its human limitation, that God had spoken; it was because he had so assumed human nature that he could be known and loved; it was in his "humiliation" that he was known for what he truly was in his innermost heart.

This faith in the fact of the Incarnation in flesh and blood, which carried with it the belief that human nature in its fullness is capable of use as an intrument or (in St. Athanasius' term) *organon* for Godhead, led immediately to a much broader conception of the meaning and value of the whole natural world than was customarily to be found among the intellectuals of the time. On the whole, the Greek philosophers and their disciples did not really think highly of the world of matter—and this was especially true during the early formative period in Christian theology. The intellectuals were concerned, in platonizing fashion, with "the eternal ideas" or with "spiritual reality"; even when they accepted matter, they tended to find a difficulty in handling and explaining it. It was indeed true that the whole Hebrew tradition had been strongly interested in maintaining the reality of the natural world and of history. But it was exactly here that the Hebrew tradition was in conflict with much if not all Greek thinking; and it was the victory of the Christian theologians in their struggle with gnosticism and docetism which guaranteed that the Hebrew world-view would have, so to say, a chance in the history of thought.

Professor Whitehead has shown that the Christian belief in the significance of the natural world and in the importance of concrete particulars within that world has been responsible for the development of science in the west; while the opposed notion, especially as found in India—whose dominant philosophy is one which denies the natural world and minimizes concrete particulars—has made the development of science a difficult if not impossible affair

wherever it is widely held. What Professor Whitehead has not seen—or at least has not said—is that
this Christian interest in the natural world and in
concrete particulars springs from the Christian faith
in the Incarnation. Indeed, it is not going too far to
assert that the possibility of and the freedom for
scientific study in the 1940's are both ultimately dependent on the victory of the Christian theologians
in the first two centuries of our era. Once the faith
in the specific Incarnation in Jesus, as involving a
true humanity, had been established, it was possible
for the Christian Church to move on; and following
the Hebrew *line of thought* while expressing much of
its theology in Greek *terms* (and neither of these
two sides of the truth ought to be overlooked in any
sound historical study or theological discussion)
eventually to come to the position of recognizing the
general incarnational and sacramental character of
the entire natural order.

That is to say, the facts which we have presented
in relation to the world and its instrumentality for
value, spirit, purpose, ideal and idea, were for Christian theology interpreted along an even more profoundly significant line. It was claimed that every
good reality expressed and declared the purpose and
being of God. Not only are truth, beauty and goodness, considered as eternal realities, expressed in the
finite world; it is truer to say that the God who *is*
among other things these values is expressed in the
world. Furthermore, the varied events of the historic process, the movements of men and nations, the
emergence of personality, the entire rich and many-
graded universe in its every range and aspect, have
all of them this revelatory function.

It is real in itself, this world; but it is a *derived*
reality, reflecting the only final Reality, God. It is

employed by God to effect his purposes. It can only be seen correctly when seen as God's field of action. Likewise God makes himself known through it in most widely various fashion. The Christian Church consistently has looked with suspicion on shortcuts or "direct contacts" with Deity, apart from the mediation of material realities, concrete and particular. It was not *denied* them, and has in fact been the mother of mysticism, but it has always maintained that such immediacy needs to be backed up by and built upon the wider mediated knowledge of God and the sacramental ways of approach to his fellowship. In other words, it has seen, with Cardinal Bérulle, that "the incarnation is the manner and mode" in which and by which God normally works in and for his creatures.

Coupled with this set of beliefs and convictions, the historic Christian tradition has regularly maintained the body-mind nature of man himself. We have already quoted extensively from St. Thomas Aquinas in our detailed discussion of this point; hence we need here only to say that on the whole it has been within the main-stream of Christian theology that thinkers have most consistently held to the duality of man as soul or mind dwelling in and using body and matter. Never, in that central tradition, has there been a denial of either side. The heresies, the sectarian theologians, small groups of "spirituals," have departed from this main stream; but the Church itself as a whole has held firmly to the view set forth classically in St. Thomas, even if some may not have liked his particular *philosophical* expression of this accepted truth.

When we turn to a consideration of the social nature of man, and the way in which he is both influenced by his tradition and also plays his part as man only insofar as he is in some sense identified with a social group and is part of a community, we discover once again that the Catholic Church has been consistent in its emphasis. The very fact that theologically the Church itself is described as "the Body of Christ" points in this direction. Besides this, the fact that it is believed (with whatever modifications may be required in order to save the statement from uncharitable exclusiveness) that "outside the Church is no salvation"—the famous Cyprianic dictum—would indicate that the central tradition of Christian theology has recognized the sociality of man as well as his materiality.

Baron von Hügel is a particularly useful guide here. His several essays on institutions and the Church, in *Essays and Addresses*, expound in admirable fashion the essential Catholic view, taking due account of recent thought on the whole subject, and building upon a sound consideration of human nature as it is in itself, but going on to show that the life of the Christian is *par excellence* life in community. As he points out, even the member of the Society of Friends, who feels that he has broken from all social dependence either for knowledge of God or for religious expression, is really unable to escape from the institutionality and sociality of life. Knowledge of the Christ in whom he believes is conveyed to him through the Church's book which is the Bible; indeed, he chooses the most ecclesiastical of the gospels (St. John) as his favorite portrait of Jesus. He inevitably takes to holding meetings, using forms of dress and speech, and employing other kinds of behavior which are expressed in communal ways. Before long, there is a new institutional expression of faith by those who deprecated such an expression as unnecessary or dangerous.

Try as hard as we can, we are unable to escape our social "conditioning." We *know* through social means and we *act* through social means. This is as true religiously as in any other way. Our ideas of religion and our religious actions, without possibility of exclusion, have their medium of impression and expression in the communal ways. And the Church, with its wealth of dogma, its liturgical formulae, its standards of conduct, is the Christian social environment and community. For Catholic theology, therefore, the essential pre-condition for a man to become a Christian is to be united with the Church, to live in it and with it, entering into its life and assimilating its faith. The tradition of Christianity *is* a tradition; it is a socially conveyed "culture," as Dr. C. C. Morrison has put it. That tradition or "culture" is a very rich and profound reality, in which the Christian must live and move and have his being, if he is to enter into the holy of holies of Christian faith.

Central to this rich social tradition is the whole sacramental idea and worship. Baron von Hügel again comes to our aid, with his argument that the belief in and worship of Jesus Christ, "God and Man, body and soul," really present in the Holy Eucharist, is the heart of Christian adoration. The genius of Christianity, in worship, is that it has recognized the facts about man and his world and has not only accommodated itself to them but has used them to bring man to God. The outward and visible signs of bread and wine, which are the ordinary commonplaces of human sustenance, are taken to be the means by which the Christian reaches to God and God reaches to the Christian. This is precisely in accord with the faith in the Incarnation itself, in that the same kind of self-giving of God which is centrally found there is believed to be carried on and made available to succeeding generations of believers as they employ the sacramental means of grace which have been provided in the Church.

Once again, the theologians of the Catholic Church have fought against all attempts to explain away the materiality of the sacrament and to make the bread and wine mere empty symbols of that which is in essence independent of them. On the contrary, the *effectuality* of the symbols, and their necessity for the strengthening and refreshing of the soul, have been an integral part of the picture. They are not incidental nor accidental to the Christian scheme of worship; they are essential to it. And to make certain that we shall come to a full understanding of this position, we may properly turn to a consideration of the sacramental system of the Church as Body of Christ, as this scheme has been described. In doing this we shall inevitably touch once more upon some of the points which have been covered at greater length in earlier chapters; but it is imperative that we do not omit them at the present point in our argument, since the cumulative effect of the whole position can thereby be brought out more satisfactorily. After this theological summary, we shall then be ready to proceed to a brief discussion of "sacramentals," those lesser "sacred signs" which have historically been employed in Christian worship, such as fire, light, water, statues, incense, vestments, *etc.*, before we conclude with a short treatment of the whole range of external religion as it makes itself felt and known in the life of the devout believer.

In regular Christian theology, the term *sacrament* can be used in a general or in a narrow sense. In the latter sense, a sacrament may be defined (in a famous sentence from Hugh of St. Victor) as "a corporeal or material element offered to the senses, which from likeness represents, from institution signifies, and from consecration contains, some invisible and spiritual grace." Four points are included in this definition—the sign, the grace, the effectual operation, and dominical institution in some proper sense. Such a four-point definition controls for the historic Church, in the main, the number of sacraments which are, so to say, ecclesiastical and thereby specifically Christian—that is, sacraments of the Body of Christ. If, on the other hand, one is concerned with the broader sense of the term sacrament, the definition given by St. Augustine is eminently satisfactory: *signum sacrum* or *signum rei sacrae*. Alternatively, the definition offered in the Catechism of the Anglican Book of Common Prayer will serve, if we stop the quotation with the opening phrases: "an outward and visible sign of an inward and spiritual grace." So soon as we go on with the Prayer Book's definition, however, and speak of the sacrament as "given unto us" and "ordained by Christ himself," we have entered into the realm of the ecclesiastical and specifically Christian sacrament. Much confusion has arisen in this connection; it is essential both to sound theology and to clear thinking—the two are necessarily one—that we maintain our distinctions.

But it is a primary condition for any satisfactory understanding of the sacraments in the Church that we be clear that these sacraments are always seen to be, from one point of view, simply special instances or particular illustrations of a general sacramental principle which is natural to the whole created order. Grace, St. Thomas Aquinas tells us, perfects nature; it does not destroy the *naturally* good creation of God but brings that creation to its intended goal in Christ and hence to its proper fruition. Thus the sacraments of the Church are not contradictory to nor a denial of the natural sacramental order; quite the contrary, for they crown and complete the order by its full and intentional infusion by and informing with divine grace in a particularly and peculiarly intensive and distinctive fashion.

The Church, we have seen earlier in this chapter, is regarded by all orthodox Christian theologians as first of all and above all the "Body of Christ." It is essential to recognize that this term is used aptly as a description of the Church, not only because St. Paul employed it, but also because it is the best and indeed the only satisfactory way of picturing the relationship of the Church to its Lord. For as in his personal humanity, Jesus Christ who is God the Word had both for his self-expression and for his evocative action among men a body that was the perfected instrument of his divine purpose, so in the social humanity which came into being through his human action and exists for the sole purpose of carrying his person and his work down through the succeeding centuries, he has a body which is in intention the perfected vehicle for his purpose and which *in its members* is on the way to increasing perfection as it more nearly becomes his vehicle.

Despite the sin, the error and the weakness of its human constituents, therefore, the Church is the Body of Christ and is itself the true sacrament of the unseen yet ever present Lord who is God-made-man. If the term "body" is to be taken as a metaphor, it must be taken very seriously as a metaphor, with the understanding that it is the only symbol adequate to express the truth about the Church. The Body of Christ is that continuing organic expression of the life of the God-Man which is informed by life-in-love because it is life-in-union; its head is the ever-living Christ; its informing life is the Holy Spirit who is the charity of God; its purpose is the incorporation of all life into Christ; its end is the return of the entire creation to God, so that he may be sacramentally expressed and active throughout the entire world-order by its free and glad surrender to him, until all shall find itself in him and he shall be all in all.

Such a view makes utterly impossible for sound Christian theology any purely mechanical or merely legal notion of the Church. One need not agree with the extremes to which Dr. Walter Lowrie found himself led many years ago, when he wrote that law and mechanical operation have no place in the Church. But one must at least agree with him in his insistence that the Church is of such a nature that organizational factors are secondary to organic. This does not at all mean that there are no mechanisms or legal arrangements which are significant in and important to the Church, any more than recognition of the human body as a totally functioning organism implies that it can possess no necessary and useful mechanisms nor conform to established norms by which it will function healthily. The historic ministry, for example, has been regarded in the Church as both a mechanism (in the sense in which we noted) and also an organic reality which is a sign of a sacred thing, namely the historic continuity of the Church and its genuine self-identity.

In our context, however, it is particularly important to stress the fact that the sacramental system of the Church, if that be a proper term at all, is a system only in the sense in which the human organism has certain systems or ways of functioning which are essential to its true health, true identity, true persistence. The sacraments of the Church are never regarded as detached from the life of the total organism, nor are they considered to work in any solely mechanical or merely legalistic fashion without that organic relationship. They do not operate apart from or in any distinction from the Body of Christ. They *are* the Body of Christ *at work*: that is their significance and their only significance.

The sacraments of the Christian Church are usually listed as seven: baptism, confirmation, the Eucharist, marriage, orders, holy unction, and penance. But the number of sacraments as so listed was reached at a comparatively late date and while it is not arbitrary it is not entirely determinative: it is at least conceivable that this number might be increased. Institution by Christ himself is the usual criterion of a sacrament of the Church. But as the result of modern biblical criticism it can hardly be affirmed with certainty that he instituted in any *formal* sense any of the sacraments, although it may be said that all were instituted by him *in genere*. That is, by general intention, and in his divine mind, he established a society in which man's salvation would be accomplished by the employment of such means of grace as properly and directly developed from his words or actions during the days of his flesh.

Furthermore, the efficacy of the sacrament depends on the divine will, given in answer to prayer but given by God and hence *assuredly* given when that is done which ought to be done to indicate the need for which the grace is the response. The sacraments, for Christian thought, depend so completely on God's will, and not on any supposed human control of God's will, that they are effective *ex opere operato.* In our more general experience in the realm of the "natural sacraments," something is done and possesses its reality apart from our response, yet it requires our response for its proper assimilation and appropriation. Similarly in the sacraments of the Church, the sacrament "works" by divine will, but requires our response so that the result may be that which the sacrament is intended to bring about. This guarantees both divine *objectivity* and human *responsibility*—the latter, too, in both senses of the word. It brings the Christian sacraments into line with our *normal* human experience in which, unless we are entirely projectionists, we recognize that human response is made to what is actually *there,* to what is really present or really done in the vast range of our social and physical environment.

A third and final consideration is that it has regularly been maintained by Catholic theology that the sacraments of the Church must be so much *of the Church* as to require a competent and recognized minister to consecrate them or perform the rite. This again relates the Christian expression of religion to the wider truths which we have already discovered concerning the social context of the general sacramental element in life.

The sacraments of the Christian Church have a singular quality in that they parallel, with amazing accuracy, the great moments and the great needs in the lives of men. As men are born into and for normal healthy living require membership in the human family, so they are baptized into the family of God. As they grow up to need strengthening for full and responsible action, so they are confirmed in order to share in the sacramental life of the Church in Holy Communion. As they fall into error and stray from the right, requiring forgiveness and reinte-

gration into society at every point, so they are
shriven and restored to the Church's fellowship in
the sacrament of absolution. As they require nour-
ishment day by day to sustain them in their human
existence, and as they desire to live nobly by offering themselves to a cause which is greater than they,
so they offer the Holy Sacrifice of praise and thanks-
giving and receive the bread of life in the Lord's
Supper. As they establish their own little human
communities of love and care, so they marry with the
blessing of God through the Church in order to set
up cells of Christian charity in the world. As they
are ill in body, and presently must die, requiring
medical care in illness and preparation for the close
of life at their final end, so they are anointed in body
when ill, and prepared for the eventual death of the
body, in the sacrament of unction. And as some of
them seek more nearly to serve high causes and to
dedicate their lives in service for the benefit of others, so in the sacrament of holy order some are set
apart for the specific vocation of ministers of the
Body of Christ.

It is the peculiar privilege of the Christian in
this main Catholic tradition of Christianity to live
as a sacramental being in a sacramental world, nour-
ished by the sacraments of the Church which is itself
the sacrament of Christ. It there were no other
proof to be offered of the truth of this Catholic position, such a parallelism as we have indicated would
seem to be almost enough to convince one. Miss
Evelyn Underhill in her striking little book *Man and
the Supernatural* wrote: "Through the Christian
sacraments that self-giving, of which the Incarnation is the supreme example, finds another and continuous expression; sense here becoming the vehicle
through which the very Spirit of life enters into the

little lives of men." So intimately, so precisely, so entirely, does this dovetail into our own general human experience, that it would be incredible for such a position as the historic Christian Catholic tradition to be other than entirely credible.

6. SACRAMENTS, SIGNS AND SYMBOLS

Our survey in this book has indicated the philosophical and psychological presuppositions of a religion which appeals to and makes use of the body and bodily action in its worship of God. Sign, sacrament and symbol have been shown to be natural to man, because he is the sort of animal who inevitably must live and move and have his being as body-mind, mind-body. They have been shown to be natural to the world in which we live, since it is a world in which value, purpose, idea and ideal, spirit and all that is implied by spirit, must be and are mediated and known through material, physical, social historic means. They have been shown to be inevitable for a Christian expression of religion, since the Christian theological outlook, the traditional development of its worship, and the intention of Christianity for men, is strongly centered in an incarnational faith. In this concluding chapter, we shall seek to say something about the whole matter of external religion, as it is expressed in the particulars of religious observance, and conclude with observations of a more general nature which may serve to emphasize once again the importance of our principle and the necessary safeguards to its implementation in practice.

The point of view for which we have argued will make the kind of worship to be found in historic Catholic Christianity a normal and natural way for men to approach God and for God to make himself known to men. Not only is this true insofar as the particular signs, symbols and sacraments denote and define Reality; it is also true in their wealth of connotation, the rich and almost undefinable aura of suggestion which they possess. For there is a certain quality of widening significance about the sacred sign which is one of its most remarkable features. In his little book, *Sacred Signs*, Romano Guardini, the German Catholic writer (who uses this term "sacred signs" so suggestively, although St. Augustine himself as we have seen earlier speaks of *signa sacra*), has made his point remarkably well. He speaks of the baptism "both in body and soul" which enables a believer to grasp "these signs as sacred signs," because they belong to the area of "doing," an area of life which (as he says) "is something elementary, in which the whole man must take his part, with all his creative powers; a live carrying-out a live experience, undertaking, seeing." It is this which enables the *whole* man and not a segment or fraction of him, Guardini remarks, to give God his due in worship, and to express "in his own bodily acts what he realizes in his soul."

As an illustration of the principle, Guardini takes the sign of the Cross. He writes: "It embraces your whole being, body and soul, your thoughts and your will, imagination and feeling, doing and resting; and in it all will be strengthened, stamped, consecrated in the power of Christ, in the name of the Holy Trinity." For, in fact, "the whole body is the tool and expression of the soul. The soul does not merely dwell in the body, as if it dwelt in a house, but it lives and works in every member and every fibre. It speaks in every line, and form, and movement of the body." From this significant assertion, Guardini proceeds to a discussion of some of the traditional "sacred signs" of Catholic worship; the sign of the

Cross, already mentioned; the use of the hand, kneeling, standing, walking, striking the breast, candles, holy water, fire, incense, ashes, bells, sacred hours and times, sacred objects (such as altars and statues, *etc.*), bread and wine, and many others, even including words themselves—which are signs of a *meaning* that cannot ever fully be expressed without them.

It is interesting to note that many who normally might not be thought to have much sympathy with Catnolic worship have come to see the importance of this particular matter. In one of our American weekly religious papers (*The Witness*), for instance, an editorial recently commended strongly the establishment of prayer-corners and the use of pictures and objects as a way of surrounding the growing child—not to mention the adult—with that atmosphere which would constantly suggest that there is, in our life, more than merely secular reality. A Lenten book by Bishop Emrich of the Diocese of Michigan, commended to the Church public by the Presiding Bishop of the Episcopal Church, has said the same, remarking that one probable reason for the loss of the keen sense of the supernatural by so many otherwise religious persons is the very fact that no suggestible objects have been about him during his formative years and that he must, in far too many instances, depend upon conceptual notions for any and all religious belief or expression.

We have already discussed the Catholic and Christian theology of sacrament, as stated in the western tradition particularly. It will be useful if before concluding we pay some attention to what are known as *sacramentals*—the term by which the theologians of the Church have designated those signs and actions, less than the recognized and ecclesiastically prescribed rites, which are yet in the same general category in that they are outward and visible signs of inward and spiritual realities. Guardini's list quoted above, is suggestive and useful to us. It may be extended or reduced, of course, but at least it does include most of the practices or objects which could be considered as "normal" in the historic Christian system. The wearing of the Cross is perhaps one of the few things which might necessarily be included but which is not explicitly discussed by Guardini.

In the practice of wearing of the Cross and other similar usages, it is unquestionably true that the principal value is in the direction of awakening and developing the religious sense in the worshiper or believer. The stress, then, is on the impressive side. In other instances, such as the bodily action of reverence towards the altar, it is obvious that the stress is on the expressive side. In each case, the important point which needs to be made, and which is often forgotten, is that the object or action in itself is not "holy" or "sacred." Even in the reverence paid to the altar, to a picture, to a statue, it is never to be forgotten that the significant truth is that the real reverence is paid to God, the *divine* object, suggested *by* and worshiped *through* the natural object. In the famous iconoclastic controversy, the insistence by St. John Damascene that the doctrine of the Incarnation demands that representation, symbolically, of holy things be permitted, was qualified however, by the declaration that it is only the divine itself which receives any worship or reverence in the strictest sense. So also in St. Thomas Aquinas, we find that the "image," about which he happens to be writing in discussing this question, is revered because of its

association with God or sacred things and not
in and for and of itself. As he says, it is by the stimulation of the senses that the mind is moved to seek
and find God: it is not *in spite of* this stimulation,
but *because of it and by reason of its operation*. And
the object which thus stimulates is itself thereby
associated in devotional practice with the God who
is being sought and found, with the grace that is
desired and received, with the help that has been
granted.

For this reason, it matters little whether the
transaction is more largely on the God-to-man side
or on the man-to-God side, more a matter of impression than of expression or of expression than
of impression. The truth remains that there is both
helpfulness and significance in the use of the various
sacred signs; and with proper theological instruction there is very slight danger of what is loosely
called "superstition" or "magic," since the divine
reality and its priority and supremacy are ever safeguarded. Indeed one may suggest that much more
serious is the opposite to the danger of superstition
arising from the use of signs, symbols and the like.
That opposite is the danger of supersession of all
spiritual awareness by a sheer this-wordly outlook—
a danger which is an all-too-present fact in our contemporary scene, and not least in those who nominally support religious institutions and presumably
have religious convictions. If there are no evocative
means provided for the supernatural, it is very likely
that the strong awareness of it will fade away, while
all the while it is being maintained that the spiritual
is being saved from contamination.

It is important also to say that the use of many
if not all of these "externals" will depend on their
personal helpfulness and usefulness to the believer.

Not everyone finds the same signs or symbols useful or helpful, although it is difficult to prescribe just what will be useful, or just what sort of person will wish to employ this or that. The practical conclusion is that individuals should be allowed to do what they wish, provided that they show no contempt for others who choose differently. And, we should add, provided also that they recognize that the wisdom of a very ancient tradition has given certain of the sacred signs a wide significance, making it likely—and *very* likely—that the average person will find them helpful. The sign of the Cross, for instance, is in our judgment hardly optional, any longer, for one who wishes to enter at all deeply into the Catholic tradition. Kneeling at the words in the Creed which describe God's humility in Incarnation, "who for us men for our salvation came down from heaven . . . and was made man," would seem to us to be demanded not only by good manners but also by the fact that the practice has proved, down the years, that it awakens and deepens, declares and expresses, as can nothing else, the awe and adoration of the Christian believer as he acknowledges God's becoming man. So likewise, reverence in the presence of the Blessed Sacrament by falling on one's knees before the most sacred of all sacred signs, would appear to be so commended to us by the age-long tradition of Christian Catholic worship, that we should hesitate a long time before refusing to adopt the practice. It is indeed very likely that the *determined* refusal to adopt it represents a deeper refusal —a refusal to accept the faith which is behind the action, that (as von Hügel expressed it) "Jesus Christ, God and Man, body and soul," is here present and self-given.

Doubtless a certain restraint in outward expression is desirable. This is especially needful in the Liturgy itself, where the very nature of the rite demands simplicity of action and directness of address. The most "ornate" celebration of the Eucharist is in truth a very simple and direct affair, as our liturgical experts have lately been reminding us. Its very glory is its colorful yet restrained suggestiveness. Effusiveness is forbidden entirely in the course of the Church's liturgical worship. But effusiveness, in the wider realm of private devotion, is another matter. It will depend so largely upon the individual that no prescriptions can be offered. One thing must be said, however—the extraordinary reserve which the Anglo-Saxon often seems to feel called upon to show in his religious life is really not any more natural to him than it would be to a Latin. Reserve is a much over-estimated quality. It can do much to ruin men's relations one with another because it impels them to refrain from exhibiting their true nature; and while this may be desirable in some respects, it is often inhibiting and self-destructive in others. William James, from the side of the secular psychologist, recognized this in his profound study of human psychology. And the more exuberant devotion of "the common people" as contrasted with the more sophisticated fear of "making an exhibition of oneself" has much to teach us at this point.

Finally, the chilly austerity of worship which fails to take account of man's real nature and its demands is responsible in large measure for the desertion of the services of the Church about which many have complained. This is no final argument for the set of ideas with which we have been concerned; but it is, on the other hand, a highly indicative consideration. There must be sound principles of church worship, there must be sound principles in personal devotional practice. This does not mean that the discussion of principles should not take account of the kind of thing which appeals to and benefits the great majority of men. Prejudices against external religion are many, but they are almost entirely ill-founded. Sincerity and earnestness, indeed, are as certainly found in external religion as anywhere else; the danger of their abuse is no greater there than elsewhere. If there is the possibility of reaching and helping many who are alienated by the cold formality of much post-reformation religion, we should do all in our power to make this possibility an actuality.

God made man and the world as they are, in the sense that it is not an accident, or a result of sin and evil, that they are compounded of matter and spirit. Presumably he wanted them to be, and likes them to be, that way. There is no reason for anyone to try to be more spiritually-minded than God.

PART TWO

Essays On Related Topics

1. THE SOCIOLOGICAL
INTERPRETATION OF RELIGION

The question of the exact nature of religion is one which has long perplexed scholars, and it is one to which many answers have been given. It would be tedious to list the hundreds—perhaps even thousands—of suggestions which have been made. But one answer to the question has for so long commanded the assent—either unreserved or qualified—of writers who are not to be dismissed as tyros, nor to be condemned as unsympathetic with religion itself, that it deserves a friendly if thorough criticism. We refer to the widely accepted "sociological theory" of the nature of religion. It may be of some value, then, to devote our attention exclusively to this theory, in an effort to discern its values and at the same time to point out its inadequacies and inaccuracies.

In our discussion, we shall give first an outline of the powerful theory which seeks to account for all religious phenomena in terms of society. After a presentation of the theory, we shall seek to make a criticism and evaluation. In our exposition of the theory we shall follow, for the most part, the writings of Emile Durkheim, the distinguished French anthropologist. The sociological view was most completely stated by him in his notable work, *The Elementary Forms of the Religious Life*. It has since been taken over by scores of anthropologists and sociologists, even by philosophers and psychologists, as the basis for their study of religion and its place in human life and society. Naturally the theory has been strongly criticized; perhaps the best analysis and attack is that of Professor C. C. J. Webb, entitled *Group Theories of Religion*. We shall use some of Dr. Webb's criticisms in the course of our concluding comments.

A convenient method of carrying out our task will be by a three-fold division. First of all, we shall consider the data and interpretation upon which Durkheim operates; then we shall present the theory which he advances to explain this material; finally, we shall offer some criticism of these views.

Our author gives us, in his most important work, a very careful analysis of the religious activities of a number of tribes, whose behavior he has studied, although Australian bushmen seem to furnish him with the major portion of his data. His first observation is that as a matter of fact, the religious observances of primitive man are almost entirely social in nature. There is no such thing, Durkheim believes, as "personal religion" on the part of the bushman; whatever religious observances he may have are of significance as belonging to the tribe, and as expressing tribal attitudes and tribal desires. At bottom, religion is a matter of cult for the tribe. Durkheim adduces instance after instance of tribal life, in which without any specific matter of belief the group join together in a ceremonial dance or in some other cultic exercise, in which they are knit as one man intent upon their activity. We have then a sense of tribal unity as one basis of religion.

It is as the result of such a tribal unity that the primitive man receives power. His purpose in uniting with his fellows in these social rites is in order to have an accession of life, which he knows occurs whenever they engage in such activities. The tribal dance brings new life and energy, and prepares the

participant for his more normal and humdrum labor.
Life, more life, fuller life—this is what the primitive
man seeks in his religious observances.

Furthermore, it is directly from these observances, and the sense of new life which comes from
them, that what we may call theologizing takes its
start. The sense of unity and the accession of new
power lead the primitive man to certain beliefs.
There is a mystery in the fact that by joining in a
dance or in a ceremonial worshipful act there comes
vitality; the savage wishes to explain what has
happened, and so the ritual is followed by the myth.
To the savage this is a quite natural procedure, and
he is under no illusions, so he feels. A tribe has lived
near some strange natural object, and engages in a
tribal dance near it or before it; there comes about
the accession of life—why? Well, the answer seems
to be simple. 'Because there is a special "concretion,"
to use Mr. Whitehead's word, of life, of power, at
that point.' But it is all relative to and comes from
the tribe and the social life in which the individual
worshiper participates and in which he loses himself.
Nor is this all—there seems to be another significant
factor, at least among numbers of tribes. The
sense of unity which is achieved in the ceremonials
and dance must come from some intimate relationship between the members of the tribe and the forces
felt to be outside them—although not outside them in
the physical sense—which pour into them during the
rite. This must be because there is a close connection
between that power and the particular tribe. Hence
the development of totemism, or the tribal symbol in
which power dwells.

Along lines similar to this, Durkheim would also
interpret the practice of sacrifice. This custom, in
which (let us say) some animal or perhaps a mem-

ber of the tribe is killed and the blood either drunk
or poured out, means that the participants in the
rite desire to share in the accession of life which is
there offered to them by actually consuming the life
of "the tribal god" or the god's representative. The
rite is social, once more, and it has for its results
unity, power, and participation in some shared life.
The primitive rites of initiation, covering a wide
range of phenomena, usually associated with pub-
erty, are also said to be of the same sort. They may
be characterized as admission to the full life of the
tribe and the giving of power so that the full life
can be shared. Again, the representative rites, in
which some god is, so to say, put through the events
of life, are likewise social in nature—they have as
their object the re-enacting of some myth (in the
Platonic sense, even for the primitive man—that is,
something believed to be truly representative of a
reality, and not just "make-believe") which unites
the tribe in one by making it share in the life-history
of its god.

So we could go on through the various phenomena of religion, taking up one of these after
another and interpreting it along the line which
Durkheim sugests. Briefly put, this line is (as we
have seen) that all religious rites of primitive man
may be understood as being social in nature, primarily of a ceremonial type, involving the developing
of a sense of tribal unity, the accession of new life,
and eventually a theologizing about such experiences
which endeavors to relate them to some wider ranges
of life, including on occasion natural phenomena.

So much for the data, or the interpretation of
the data, upon which Durkheim builds his theory of
the nature of religion. Now for the theory itself. We
have noted carefully the emphasis which Durkheim

lays on the social nature of religion among primitive men. He takes this as the basis for his theory of religion. Religion, in the last analysis, he believes, is not merely expressed in social ways; it *is* a social life. That is, it is the life of the tribe expressing itself in certain observable ways. It is by this union of the members of a group in the common worship, in the dance or the ceremonial, that there comes a sense of oneness in purpose—the individual as such does not count, but is lost in the larger purpose of the whole group. Secondly, it is from this social activity that there comes the sense of new life. When men engage in some common act, working themselves up to a sufficient pitch of physical vigor and spiritual enthusiasm, they have what has been called, vulgarly, "spiritual second-wind"— a feeling that they are being sustained and carried along by a life which is larger than their own, which flows into them and strengthens and develops their own relatively undeveloped life. Then, when there is this sense of new life, in the unity of the tribe, there comes about also a feeling of oneness not only with the tribe itself, but also with nature.

Upon this complex event, sooner or later (very much later, indeed, in Durkheim's view) man's rational faculty gets to work. What is to explain the experience? The primitive man constructs a myth which will explain it—that is, he says that the new life comes from fellowship with, communion with, some tribal god—the totem—or some force which inheres in objects; and so he constructs a kind of theology, or at least an attempted explanation of his "religious experience." But, says Durkheim, while his experience is perfectly real and valid, his construction or explanation is wrong. For in the long run, theology is nothing more or less than sociology.

The basis of the religious experience is not something external to human society, but is simply human social life at its intense level. There is, he says, no external object, no reality corresponding to the totem or the mana-conveying presence—that is objectification, so to speak, of the actual experiences of the tribe itself, when it is functioning as a unity in religious exercises. In the words of a modern American writer, what is real is only the spirit (and that with a lower-case "s") of the tribe. There is no adequate reason, given in religious experience, to predicate an "outside," trans-human or trans-social reality. Therefore, applying Occam's razor ("entities are not to be multiplied beyond necessity") Durkheim says that there is no need to call in the hypothesis of a god to explain religious experience. It can adequately be described and explained in terms of social experience.

Such is the theory of the French anthropologist. But will it hold water? We may say one thing quite plainly: it is not possible to dismiss it in the cavalier manner in which some writers have dismissed it. At any rate, such a distinguished scholar as Professor Whitehead is prepared to adopt this view of the *origin* (but not of the *nature*) of religion; and he has argued for it at length and with a wealth of material in his *Religion in the Making;* and many other anthropologists have been convinced that there is much to be said even for the theory itself. But is it adequate?

In the first place, it seems, one may point out that the fact that primitive religion seems to be social in its every aspect does lend very powerful support to Durkheim. And there is no disproving his statements here. Primitive religion is almost entirely a matter of tribal cultus, of ritual dance, of ceremonial. But to say this is merely to state a fact, and not to give an explanation. Why do savages go through these strange gyrations? It is here that Durkheim seems to fail us. He can outline the theologies of the primitives, and then can criticize them quite effectively. But he does not tell us why man does this sort of thing in the first place. He does it to have access of life; yes, of course—but why did he start doing it at all? Did he just happen to join with his fellow tribesmen one day, and just happen to do some kind of a dance, and then just happen to notice new life and power and unity and all the rest of it? This seems quite improbable. A much better explanation would be that something strange outside him—some natural object, some extraordinary event, called from him some sentiment of—yes, we must say it—reverence, yet strangely drew him; and he and his fellows, in order to express this sentiment, engaged in their dance or rite—unwittingly, unknowingly, but in fear or awe of something which they could not understand but which attracted even while it repelled them. They tried to reproduce something that they had seen, or they adopted their natural social reactions to that external reality, and approached it by some transmuted social act. So we are driven behind Durkheim's purely social explanation, back to the conceptions of mana and tabu.

We may also enquire about this explanation of religion from a somewhat more advanced viewpoint. Religion has been predominately social; but there have come times when against the background of sociality it has been individual with a vengeance—as with the Old Testament prophets, or perhaps with Martin Luther and his "Here I stand; I can do no other, God help me." *God* help *me*. Can that be explained on Durkheim's theory? The sociological explanation will go along very well; but when we get individual assertion (the sense that there is something of a personal relation of the man to his god) the theory falls to the ground. Luther, and the prophets, are by intention standing out against their tribe, against the social customs; and they are calling on something outside that tribe to defend them, to back them up, in their opposition. That is how religion *developed,* from the most primitive times; and one feels that a theory of the nature of religion which is unable to explain its development and purification through the centuries, does not really take one very far.

Again, from a philosophical viewpoint, is social life itself a self-explanatory matter? As an integral part of the universe out of which they emerge, men do have some relationship to that universe. Their social life is not something that floats about, entirely dissociated from the world. It is in some sense a manisfestation of that world. Human experience, even in its most social aspects, is not experience only of human relations; it has its roots in, and its connections with, the total environment, from which it cannot cut itself loose. In truth, it is always, in its degree, trans-social; just as it is always, in some degree, trans-subjective. Do we know anything more than our own thoughts; or the thoughts of our neighbors? Is there any reality outside us to which we respond, or which responds to us? In the non-religious spheres, we are certain that this is so; can we refuse to admit it in the sphere of religion?

Perhaps these suggested arguments against Durkheim will indicate that there is more to be said about religion than that it is a kind of intensified social experience of man. But when we have said that, we must not forget that there is much truth in what Durkheim says. The religion of Israel gives us abundant evidence: take the familiar story of the battle of the Jews with the Canaanites, reflected in the Song of Deborah—the accession of new power, the sense of unity, the feeling that nature is with man—all this is found there. But nature is with man, not merely by projection, but in some unfathomly deeper sense; and it is nature with a capital "N." For the explanation of the enriched social experience, the intensified personal energy, is found in that belief that some reality which is more than man and his social life, even though akin to him and it, has been with him, and has entered into his life and worked through him to achieve certain ends. That is the conviction of the early Israelites. Something like it, even if vastly dimmer, may be found in the primitive savage theologizing that he has found a new sense of oneness with his tribe; he has found a new power in his own life; he has achieved some strange union with nature, because through his deepest social experience Reality has made its impact upon him and his tribe, and in devious and hidden ways has worked upon them and revealed itself to them.

2. RELIGION AND MORALITY

I

A story heard the other day will be useful for the discussion of the subject of this essay. A Protestant minister, runs the tale, met a Roman Catholic priest on a village street. In the course of their conversation it developed that they had different ideas on their ministerial function, expressed in the two phrases attributed to them. "My job," said the Protestant, "is to try to make good people religious." "Mine," said the Roman Catholic, "is to try to make religious people good."

Now, however one may like or dislike the particular distribution of terms in this story, the point which it makes is a useful one. That point is, simply, that there is a real distinction between religion and morality. The fact of that distinction is frequently obscured, especially in a religion like Christianity, in in which the moral consequences of religion are so integral to the whole picture that they are sometimes identified with the thing itself. But the fact is there, and it needs to be stressed, although we ought never to be satisfied with an unethical religion or with an irreligious morality.

In a day now somewhat past, there was a movement for the re-writing of the creeds in what were called "moral terms." It was felt that the ancient credal formulae were unfortunate in that they did not stress sufficiently the ethical element in religion.

But Dr. William Temple, the late Archbishop of Canterbury, in discussing this idea, gave the proper answer when he said that a creed which was concerned with ethics would be a creed that developed hypocrites—people who claimed moral goods which in fact they did not attain. The function of a creed, he remarked, was to state the revelation of God and our belief in it; the ethical consequences should follow as a matter of course, but they were not part of religious beliefs *as such*.

Likewise, long before Temple's comment, the great von Hügel in his discussion of the nature of religion, protested that it was concerned with "is-ness," not with "oughtness"; with the fact of God and the recognition of God by his creatures, and not with their moral obligations in the light of that fact and its recognition. Morality, he insisted, is different from religion, although in the highest religions it is closely connected and inescapably involved in the properly religious life. Religion is primarily "adoration"; mortality is primarily "obligation."

Nor does such a position for a moment militate against the assumption that the divine judgment of man is in terms of man's total behavior, rather than of man's specific religious response. Doubtless religion is not important to God in himself; *he* does not have one! Hence he must and will judge men preeminently in their moral life—its integrity, purity and reality. But for us men, religion is very important; *we* must have one. We must have one, because the condition of our sane, wholesome living—and hence, of our moral behavior, as well—is an attitude towards, an aprehension of, and a place in, the total scheme of things such as will give meaning and dignity to human existence. And in the long run, religion alone is able to give this.

There is a very immediate and practical reason for an insistence on the distinction between religion and morality—a reason which ought to be obvious in our own day. For a long time, now, the ordinary American has tended to identify Christianity with a certain ethical standard. This has broken down into two kinds of morality. One is the rather negative ethic of an older generation, but still a powerful force. Some one has characterized it as the "Don't drink, don't smoke, don't dance morality." The other is the positive but somewhat generalized morality of a younger generation, a morality which might be characterized as the "Do good and serve others morality."

Vast numbers of folk are unable to accept the first, at least in its obvious negative sense, while towards the second they take the attitude of admiring the intention but wondering about its actual helpfulness in concrete situations. In either case, they have so identified this morality with Christianity that they feel that, if they cannot actually attain to the ethical standard which is as they believe demanded of them thereby, they have no right to have a religion at all, or at least to be Christian. Furthermore, they critize those who are members of the religious comunions on the ground that *they* do not fully attain the moral standard which is, supposedly, identical with Christianity itself. Lastly, professing Christians are themselves dubious, now and again, as to whether *they* have any right to continue as Christians, when their behavior is all too often below that which ideally is required of them.

II

It is plain to any historian of religion that the

general idea of religion in America is of the "sect" rather than the "church" type, to use Troeltsch's convenient distinction. The notion is that religion is for the special and holy *few*, who are perfect followers of their chosen way, rather than for the sinful *many*, who may find help towards goodness and incentive towards moral effort within a fellowship that comes into being on other grounds. The latter, or "church" view, regards the Christian fellowship not as a "museum for saints," but as a "hospital for sinners," as the old slogan puts it. The former makes moral perfection, or the near achievement of it, an implied *condition* of membership, even if in recent times the ideal has broken down and the "saints" seem fewer in number.

Historically, it seems that there can be no question that Christianity down the ages has not been in the first instance a moral system. Morality has been extremely important, but the *first* emphasis has been put elsewhere. Christianity has been a *religion*, centering about the action of God in Jesus Christ; the response in faith and worship to that figure; the dedication of life to him and the empowering of life by him; the transfiguration of personality by his active love and the establishment of a hope for continued personal existence because of his victory over death and sin. It has been a religion embodied in a community, by which the action of God in Christ has been extended down the centuries and made a vital factor for succeeding generations. It has been a religion in which, therefore, community replaces "solitariness," for which the Bible itself has been a parable—for the Bible begins with man alone in a garden, and ends with man in a city as one of a company of redeemed brethren.

The result of this religion, in its communal expression, has been a morality that is both humanist and rigorist, both generous and exacting. But the general trend of the Christian movement has been to find the Christian ethic a real practicable one for men, in the degree to which they have truly and wholeheartedly "belonged" to the fellowship, and not *vice versa*. As Dr. Fosdick once put it, Christianity historically has said that "we *ought*, because we *are*." We ought to act like Christians, because by the divine action we have become and now are Christians —that is, we are of the company of the disciples and servants of the Lord Jesus Christ.

One is thoroughly convinced, when one looks about, that so far as the questing, ill-adjusted, unsatisfied youth of our time are concerned, not to speak of their elders, they will be won to Christianity by this kind of an approach rather than by a strictly ethical one. For those who are within the Christian fellowship, on the other hand, a stirring to action of a moral kind is essential. *They* need to be roused to a realization of the ethical demands of the faith which they profess and the worship which they offer. But for the others, our primary task is to present Christianity as a faith, a religion, which makes sense of life, gives dignity to life and provides power for life. We should welcome them into the fellowship, not because they are morally good but because they are spiritually lost. We should preach our faith as God's gospel of deliverance from alienation, from lost-ness; as the assurance that "underneath are the everlasting arms" and the promise that "all shall be well," as Mother Julian of Norwich said, because "God made, God loves and God keeps" his word. Then, *when* we have so won them, we should be rigorous in the moral demands which our faith makes but also humanist in recognizing that men are weak and not only may but will sin, as things are—or, in other words, that despite their labors they will fail to achieve continually the kind of living which is natural to "the man in Christ."

We have long been delivered from the idea that *ecclesiasticism* is the Christian religion, although we know that the *ecclesia*, the Church, is fundamental to it. We have lately been delivered from the idea that *biblicism* is the Christian religion, although we all know that the Bible is the central, classical and normative expression of our faith, in terms of its origin and its formative period. We ought also to be delivered from the idea that *ethicism* or *moralism* is the Christian religion, even while we insist that a wide and high and deep morality is involved in Christianity.

III

All men are *implicitly* religious, even if they do not possess in a marked degree the so-called "religious instinct." By this we mean that all men have a desire to "make sense" of their lives, to ground their being upon the "unconditioned," to be related to the fundamental drive in the universe. They may not express this in specifically religious ways; it is, none the less, the only adequate explanation of their behavior and their labor—as Dr. Paul Tillich has so admirably shown in his book *The Religious Situation*. On the other hand, men do not naturally and immediately (apart from the religious community) achieve a morality which is consonant with high religion. That is why the Roman priest's remark quoted at the beginning of this essay, is more adequate than the Protestant minister's: "My job," said the priest, "is to try to make religious people good."

There is no reason, however, that the Roman Catholic should make this claim exclusively. *All* high religion, Catholic and Protestant, is or ought to be in a like case. The job of the parish priest and minister is *first* of all to introduce men to God in his holiness, his love and his forgiveness. *Then*, and only then, can he rightly and intelligently talk about moral requirements made by that God. For then, and only then, is the context right for such requirements. It is to those of us who are *within* the community that the moral imperative needs to be preached; but it will not have much effect upon us if we are without some real and basic religious adjustment.

Furthermore, it is of the essence of the life of a religious tradition to be a life "in discipline." That is, ascetical theology and its practical implications are an integral part of the whole Christian as of every other religious complex. This is why in the Catholic communions, as our own Anglican Church, the sacrament of penance or absolution has been available. It is also why the Methodists were strongest when they had the old "class meeting," why the Oxford Groups re-discovered the practice of confession, and why all vital religion has been concerned to recognize men as sinners, to encourage them to confess the fact, and to give them strength to begin again and again the moral life which their faith demands but which their practice so sadly fails to achieve in its fullness. A distinguished Protestant minister in New York City has said frankly that for want of some such contemporary discipline, vast numbers of religious people are "frustrated and beaten" in their lives. On the other hand, for want of a religious orientation, the moral struggle of the professed "humanist" becomes in its way a frustration, too. The increasing interest in "religion and health" amongst the non-professionally religious, as Dr. Seward Hiltner has lately pointed out (*American Scholar*, Summer 1946), illustrates this admirably.

No matter how carefully one guards oneself, misunderstanding is always possible in a discussion of this sort. Therefore let us conclude by repeating that we are not for a moment denying the moral demands of Christianity, nor suggesting that they are unimportant or negligible. We are insisting on something quite different, something about which Kierkegaard had much to say that is invaluable for us. The Christian faith comes *first;* the morality of the Christian tradition comes *second*. But the second is a *real* second; it comes *directly* after the first. When Kierkegaard remarked that the religious category "dethrones" the ethical as well as the æsthetic, he did not mean that it annihilated it. It appears that some people cannot understand the difference between the two! He meant precisely what he said: that religion is primary, with morality as an utterly essential corollary.

For a Christian, anyway, there can be no unethical religion nor irreligious morality, as we said at the beginning. The writer to the Hebrews put it for us, with the correct order of things, "The God of peace, that brought again from the dead our Lord Jesus, that great shepherd of the sheep, through the blood of the everlasting covenant, make you perfect in every good work to do his will, working in you that which is well pleasing in his sight, through Jesus Christ; to whom be glory for ever and ever. Amen."

3. CHRISTIANITY AS A CULTURE

We are just now recovering from a long period of time during which, both within and without organized Christian bodies, it was thought that when one said "Christianity" one meant a particular ethical code, either directly taught by Jesus Christ or at any rate implied in his teaching and example. Countless numbers of our contemporaries still regard Christianity as "a way of life" in this sense; and they accept or reject it as being a possible, or an ideal, or a useful, or an absurd, or an irrelevant ethical code.

In the reaction from this position, many of our theologians and most of our younger clergy are inclined to present Christianity today as a system of belief. The Christian position is essentially an affirmation of the "meaning" of things, they would say; it is given in the form of doctrinal assertions or in terms of historical events with their consequences for our belief about God and man. This conception of Christianity, now the vogue in seminaries which were formally known as "liberal," is maintained by the "neo-orthodox" school; it has not yet managed to win the general public, either within or without the organized religious bodies, but it has of course always been the contention of the strongly conservative elements in Christendom.

There is still another notion of the meaning of Christianity, not so commonly accepted in the Protestant circles in this country, but current in the Anglican Communion and sweeping over the Roman

Catholic world. This is the view that Christianity is in essence a mode of worship. It implies the elements of faith and ethical behavior but it is pre-eminently an action in adoration of God, conceived, of course, in terms of the Christian epic. The liturgical revival in recent years has stressed this for Episcopalians and for Roman Catholics. Today its influence is spreading to other bodies, as is shown by the renewed interest in the church year, the sacrament of the Lord's Supper as the central Christian service of worship, and the already familiar concern for more "worshipful" church buildings.

It is not the purpose of this essay to deny the truth and value of any of these three conceptions of Christianity. Each one of them, indeed, is both true and valuable. But the tendency to insist on a choice among them, and then to center attention upon the selected conception as exclusively correct, is mistaken and dangerous, as well as thoroughly misleading from an historical point of view. Christianity, in its fullness, includes a set of affirmations concerning the "meaning" of things, based upon historical events and explicated in firm statements of belief, as it also includes a mode of worship by which believers are related to God through participation in the Christian event or epic, and a kind of moral code which is implied in and demanded by the impact of Jesus Christ upon human life. But the deeper truth is that Christianity is all these things—*and more*.

What is the *more* which Christianity essentially is? It is a social heritage embodied in a community. It is a tradition, a handing-down of certain habits of believing, worshiping, acting. It is, in fact, a "culture"—by which we mean a totality of outlook and activity wherein what a man believes and what

he does—not to speak of how he worships God—are
so closely and intimately inter-related, so directly and
immediately at one, that it is impossible to hold to
one without the others. One might say then that
Christianity *is* the Church—if by the Church we
mean the *Una Sancta*, the fellowship of loving souls
who look to and find their life in Jesus Christ understood as God's supreme action in history, and also
those who, peripheral to the fellowship, are in any
way touched or influenced by that impact.

Now the theologians will very likely, and correctly, put it in this form: As Jesus Christ is the divine
arrival in history, in unprecedented and supreme
fashion, so likewise the Church which sprang into
being as a response to that arrival is the divine community which (as St. Paul said) is the Body of
Christ. As the Body of Christ it is the carrier of
Christ down the centuries and across the continents
to all men everywhere. The fact of Christianity is the
fact of Christ in his Church. The fact of Christian
discipleship is the fact of membership in the Body
of Christ. But the ordinary non-theological Christian
will wonder what all this means in his own life. And
it is precisely at this point that our contemporary renewal of the sense of churchmanship is defective. It
is just here that the re-awakening of orthodoxy all
around us is weakest.

For in the last resort it matters very little
whether we have the correct theological understanding of the nature of the Church and of its
centrality in Christianity, if we have not realized in
our own experience the meaning of our membership,
which Baron von Hügel (in his delightful phrase already quoted in this volume) quaintly called
"churchly appurtenance." Nor does the recognition
that Christianity is a religion, with firm convictions

that cannot be compromised despite the necessary and invaluable effort to restate the faith in new terms, mean very much unless the convictions are vividly and vitally related to the totality of life which each disciple knows and experiences.

Progress towards an answer and some help for the average layman can be had only if we understand that in a "culture" like Christianity—an integral community of faith, worship and life—the presence of the several different aspects or elements will modify one another. For example, the convictions about God and man which are part of the Christian faith will be different from the usually held intellectual convictions of non-Christian folk when once it is seen that they are grasped most satisfactorily— indeed alone grasped satisfactorily—in the act of worship, and that they require implementation in daily living. Likewise, worship itself will be a deeper and more sustaining reality when it is at every point understood in terms of basic belief, so that the ancient adage *lex orandi lex credendi* comes alive in our personal participation.

This is why so many of us are certain that the Lord's Supper, the Holy Communion, the Eucharist, the Mass (call it what you will) is the specifically characteristic Christian action in worship. Here, and here uniquely and normatively, the *sense* of Christianity is apprehended, not in an intellectual fashion nor as an intellectual matter but as a living experience. But unless this action leads, as rightly it must, to a renewal and strengthening of Christian character it is sterile. So worship is conditioned by, and in its turn modifies, both faith and life.

Supremely this fact of Christianity as a social "culture" is illustrated in the question of Christian behavior. The other day a friend remarked that a certain mutual acquaintance was a "fine Christian," although in truth we both knew that the person under discussion was religiously an agnostic, whose life was lived entirely on secularistic and humanistic assumptions. Here is a classic example of misapprehension. Undoubtedly the gentleman is a good and moral citizen. Equally certain is it that a theist would be bound to acknowledge that a man's admirable moral character depends, in spite of his own non-theistic assumptions, on the hidden but real operation of God, the indwelling but concealed power and purpose in his life. Surely, too, there must be marked resemblances in actual deed between his conduct and that of a Christian believer, if only because he lives in a society which still has some traces of Christian morality. But the essential quality which makes behavior Christian is lacking in him.

For a Christian is one whose behavior reflects that "in-formation" of his personality by Christ which can alone be known in the community of faith where Christ is accepted as God's visitation to men and his grace vitally assimilated in worship as the sustaining power of the inner life. This is the reason that we can rightly say that one whose moral conduct is less than perfect is still a Christian, if he lives "in Christ" by virtue of membership in the community; while we must on the other hand refuse the adjective Christian in its normative sense to even the best of those whose life is lived apart from Christ. Nor does this deny the possibility of ultimate salvation for the latter, any more than it assures it to the former. That is in God's hands, and in his hands alone. Refusing the Christian name to these people is simply a recognition of the facts in their plain historical meaning. It is a way of saying that the task of the Church is to make Christian people good, rather than just to make good people Christian.

Christianity, then, is a credal, liturgical and ethical religion. But it is a religion, first of all. And a religion is a bond between man and the source of his life who is God. The Christian religion, by its very nature, is such a bond established and secured in a community which is rich in faith, in worship and in moral implications. Such a position has tremendous consequences. Educationally, for instance, it demands that we teach Christianity in such a fashion that children grasp it as a set of fundamental beliefs, experience it as an act of worship and live it as a moral code. We can never hope to make the younger generation Christian unless we give them the *wholeness* of "the Christian thing." Years ago we gave them beliefs only. Nowadays we tend to be concerned simply with "attitudes," which is to say, with moral implications. But we shall fail unless these two, *and* Christian worship as the vitalizing element in the whole, are in our picture. Even then we shall fail unless we lead the young to understand Christianity in its totality, as meaning that one belongs to a specific form of "culture" which is different from secular or non-Christian society, and which therefore includes intellect, emotion and will within its operational field.

A final example. The total outlook of many, perhaps most, of our young people today is not Christian. They do not grasp Christianity as a rich whole, including a set of beliefs about the nature of things, and hence determinative of thought; nor do they experience it in vital worship, and hence find it empowering of personality. In the result, the specifically Christian teaching about life in its ethical aspect is uprooted from its basis in conviction about the nature of things, and is taught without adequate recognition of the grace of God which can lift man above the level of mere desire to the level of divinely inspired and divinely assisted desire. Why then should we be surprised at the appalling lowering of the moral standard?

What we require today is a preaching and teaching of integral Christianity—and not a preaching only, but a living of it. To be a Christian means to be a member of a community brought into existence by God's act in Christ. And that means to learn to live within and reflect the unique faith, worship and life which are the characteristic marks of a distinctive and unique "culture."

4. CHRISTIANITY AND THE SEXUAL *MORES*

This essay is concerned with a particular aspect of Christian ethics. It does not pretend to discuss the larger social problems which are involved, nor to indicate the wider social implications as to the total task of the Christian Church. To do this—even to attempt to do this—would open up a field so vast that a whole series of essays, or more likely a series of books, would be required. Our interest at the moment is in one thing alone: the current sexual *mores*, obtaining through the length and breadth of the land, in relationship to what we venture to call the Christian "culture."

Very likely the writer ought not to speculate on this subject at all. As a theologian, he should "stick to his last" rather than risk entering the field of ethics or moral theology. Certainly he can claim no particularly expert knowledge which would qualify him to speak with particular authority on the subject. On the other hand, it is precisely as a theologian concerned with the doctrinal or dogmatic side of the Christian tradition, that he has come to feel the marked divergence between what is implied in Christianity, in regard to sexual behavior, and the commonly accepted point of view today on this matter. Any thoughtful Christian has the right and the duty to bring to the subject such insight and understanding as he may possess; especially important is a consideration of this topic from the dogmatic side, since this appears to be almost entirely neglected in most discussions of sex.

111

By now we who are whole-heartedly devoted to what may be termed "an integral Christianity" ought to recognize the fact that we do not live in a Christian country. By "integral Christianity" is meant a total world-view, which includes a set of assumptions about the purpose of human life and its enduring values; a method of adjustment to the eternal environment of human life which for Christian faith is the divine Reality; and a mode of behavior and quality of life which, with whatever imperfections and inadequacies in practice, are regarded as demanded by the assumptions and empowered by the adjustment. Christianity, so understood, is a socially conveyed tradition, embodied in a community or Church which is all-embracing in its significance and which brings to the several members thereof their unique and special significance as Christians.

Those who are Christians in this historical sense may not realize to the full, in their day-by-day living, everything that is implied in their membership in the community which is the Body of Christ. The fact that they are in "a state of spiritual insufficiency" as men means that even when that insufficiency is supplanted by the sufficiency potentially available and actually conveyed in the Body of Christ, they will still be possessed by a "hang-over," a tendency to self-interest and imperfection which persists even amongst "the redeemed." This theology calls concupiscence. But if members of the Church do not realize in practice their high calling, they do know or should be brought to know the standards of Christian behavior, the assumptions behind that behavior and those standards, and the devotional techniques which serve, among other things, as an aid to Christian living.

He would be a bold man who would claim that the generality of our people, even including many nominally within the Church, are truly "integral Christians." More than half of our population is not even connected with organized Christianity by outward profession. They may do lip-service to Christian "principles" and "ideals"; their generosity may sometimes shame the professing Christian. But in truth their thinking is dominated by assumptions which are not integrally Christian, whatever value otherwise they may possess. And quantities of church people are so permeated by the secular assumptions of our age that their church membership does not result in much more than a vague acceptance of what they conceive to be "Christian idealism."

It is not fair to use the men and women who have lately served in our armed forces as a kind of illustration for any and every observation. Yet it is the fact that because our army and navy were recruited by a general conscription, they did represent a cross section of the life and thought of younger America and indeed of the whole American mind and behavior. Hence it is worth our notice that chaplains generally told us that the men and women in the armed forces, brave and splendid as they were in so many ways, were not to any marked degree permeated by Christian thinking, nor were their standards of conduct markedly "conditioned" by their explicit or implicit assumption of the truth of the Christian position.

With this in mind, let us turn to the question of the sexual *mores*, as they relate to historical Christianity.

II

Christianity has a definite and unique view of sex in human life. Man, it holds, is a mind-body complex; his personality or self must be expressed through his physical structure. In his mind-body complex, the fundamental drive is towards fulfilment in an *other*; that is to say, man is so created that he seeks for love, but he is also so created that he goes out of himself in love towards the *other*. His psychological structure, like his physiological, is such that this love-drive must normally find bodily expression; his whole organism, indeed, is ordered for expressing the love-drive.

But man is *man*, not simply a beast. He is to realize his true *end*, his manhood, by an ordered and rightly directed expression of all his powers. In the area of sexual life, under God who is man's final end as well as his creator, there is such a right ordering. This is the realization of bodily love, so far as love is to find bodily expression in him, in spiritual love which under God implies life-long union with a single partner, rather than promiscuously and without control or direction. Bodily love may be sublimated (as by the "religious" in the sense of monks and nuns) so that its validity is guaranteed but its channel is altered; it may not be destroyed or totally frustrated without serious damage to personality. Equally serious damage is done, however, when this bodily love is expressed through departures from its intended spiritual meaning; these deviations are contrary to God's will because they are contrary to that normal development of manhood which is needful for man's essential God-given nature. God's will for man is not imposed arbitrarily and externally, but is ordained as the truest and best way in which, in and under God, fullness of human development can be accomplished.

The physical side of sexual life, therefore, is "good." It is part of God's created order and within his purpose. It is natural to man's self-realization as God's creature. It is the supreme thing about man as an animal. Its meaning, in spiritual regard, is to be the sacramental expression of his spiritual nature, giving itself to and finding personality in an *other*. When love, so understood, is related to the "unconditioned" in life—that is, to God—it is a sharing in the very life of God himself, although necessarily in an analogous fashion. It is a sharing in self-giving and self-completion through self-giving. Furthermore, it is a marriage of bodies which normally results in another sharing—this time, in God's work by *pro*-creation, acting as God's agent under God and by his power in further creative action.

Such a conception of sex is integrally Christian. To sustain it, the entire Christian position must be assumed; to approach its realization in actual experience, the love of God given through the sacramental life of the Body of Christ is indispensable. To depart from it, for a Christian, is sinful; while for those outside the life of the Christian community sex is almost inevitably frustrating and self-defeating, because it lacks that total meaning and that place in a pattern which the Christian faith alone can give.

III

Now how far do such ideas play a part today in the thinking of the average citizen? We do not mean a conscious part; we mean a tacit, implicit part, as something assumed and almost unconsciously "lived by"? Unless one's observation is entirely mistaken, almost no part. It ought to be acknowledged honestly that the sexual *mores* of our time are not in fact predicated on any such set of beliefs.

An illustration is in point here. We have lately been informed that by the time they are twenty-one, six to eight males of our American youth probably have had sexual experience of some type, while amongst young women the figure is probably four to six. This, with other information, has been given in an article by Chaplain George Tittman of the United States Army, in an article in *The Witness* for February 9, 1946. The Chaplain remarks that the young person who has not had some experience, intimate or otherwise, before twenty-one is the exception and not the rule. The important point is that the considerations which govern this experience are almost never those of "Christian culture." On the contrary, they are more likely to be pleasure, temporary satisfaction, thrill, perhaps convention. A recent discussion with a young man disclosed to the writer that even for a sincere Christian there could be a total separation in his thinking between genuine Christian faith and sexual behavior. The youth was in no sense promiscuous; he had felt, however, no departure from his Christian profession when he had sexual relations with a girl in whom he happened to be deeply interested, if she were willing; neither had he felt that approaches to such intimacy, as a way of enjoying a "date," could be in any way blameworthy in a Christian. It was only after a Christian position on sex such as that outlined above had been presented to him, that he saw that sexual behavior had some direct relationship to his deep Christian faith, and he expressed gratitude for what he called a "more beautiful view" of the matter than he had previously known.

This story will indicate at least one course of action demanded from the Christian Church. So far as concerns those who, like this young man, are "of the household of faith," it is our plain duty to teach the total Christian position in such a way that sexual behavior is seen as part of the pattern. Christian instruction in sexual matters is as much part of our program of religious education as the significance of Easter. Christianity must be "taught" and "caught" as an integral tradition, in which belief, worship and practice are so united that they involve and imply one another. How this is to be done, in sexual matters, is a question for religious educators, if the Christian view of life is to be preserved at all.

IV

But right here there is a danger. There is the possibility of a puritanical attitude which will simply be shocked at sexual aberrations. This is thoroughly unchristian. For the Christian Church is aware—and individual Christians ought to be aware also—of the patent, regrettable and shameful fact that men sin. We cannot welcome sin nor condone it. But we must *understand* the sinner and then seek to re-integrate his life, by God's grace, in accordance with his true end and his ultimate destiny.

If man is so pre-eminently a being "made for love" both spiritually and physically, as Christianity insists he is, it is almost bound to follow, because man is a sinner—with a tendency to easier and more obvious ways of self-realization, as we have seen—

and even when redeemed in the community of the faithful is still prone to sin, that he may permit himself to find less exacting way of seeking a physical satisfaction for what is in its essence, although often unconsciously, a spiritual drive. Therefore he must be helped to the true insight, the Christian standard, which maintains the inter-relationship of physical and spiritual. He must not simply be condemned as hopeless because so often, even in Christian circles, he falls. With our current *mores* surrounding him, it is very likely that he will fall, until and unless he has been sufficiently integrated into the total Christian "culture" so that Christ is truly "formed" in him.

Furthermore, Christian counselling needs to be more widely available and more realistic, to help young people and others in their sexual relationships. Far too often this has not been at hand for professing Christians. Mrs. Grace Overton, in a recent book on this subject, has said that help is needed particularly in the matter of "amorous play," popularly known as "petting." The subject has been dismissed with horror or its prevalence minimized. But it is very real and very present, as anyone acquainted with young people knows. The Christian counselor should be ready to raise the discussion of the practice to the level of Christian *norms* rather than sheer physical *desire*. We need, indeed, what might be called "a moral theology of 'petting.'" And in addition to the theory, we need a practical casuistry to help young people in handling their problem, without flat condemnation on the one hand or mere condoning on the other. If this suggestion seem scandalous to some, they should consider the traditional Christian moral scheme in its handling of many not dissimilar questions.

This is within the context of the Christian fellowship. But it is only within that context that this essay is concerned to make suggestions. Perhaps some qualified person can follow with a consideration of the best method of handling the situation outside the fellowship of faith. Obviously the *best* method is the conversion of America to Christianity, in an integral sense. Short of that, some program should be devised which Christians, along with all "men of good will," can support in an effort to raise the sexual standard. The writer would defend, for his part, a revived emphasis on "the law of nature" as common ground for non-Christians. Others may have other suggestions.

One thing is clear. Christians have a position on the meaning of sex in human life which must unfalteringly be maintained, no matter what secular society may say or do. Perhaps the blatant renunciation of that Christian position, with its particular assumptions, by our secular American society may force us to a new realization of Christian demands. As members of Christ's Body we are (in the New Testament phrase) "a peculiar people," with a total "culture" different from that which obtains in what the New Testament calls "the world." It is only when this difference is realized freshly and vividly, that we can usefully go on to recognize, gladly and generously, the approximations to Christian faith and practice in other places. To be a Christian means, in sexual as in other matters, to be *something*, to have a definite position which is declared and so far as human frailty and sin permit, practiced.

A former President of Princeton University, Dr. Francis Landey Patton, once remarked: "When you take from *anything* that which makes it *something*, what you have left is *nothing*."

5. DOES GOD MAKE
ANY DIFFERENCE?

Many of us recall the saying of Carlyle, who cried out about God, "He *does* nothing, he *does* nothing!" It was an angry but yet a despairing cry. Its meaning reduces to the proposition that the doctrine of God is irrelevant to man in his need and in his perplexity. We Christians certainly would not agree with Carlyle. We are clear that belief in God makes a profound difference. Furthermore, and much more important, we are clear that God *does* do something in the world. In fact we are sure that the world is the sphere of his most intimate and direct as well as of his general and pervasive operation. But that many people can still have the feeling which Carlyle expressed seventy-five years ago is a commentary on the imperfection of our Christian affirmation of the truth about God, as well as an illustration of the failure of Christians to exemplify in life the difference which belief in God does make.

Let us then consider certain of the important contributions which the doctrine of God makes to our thought and our action as we find ourselves situated today in a world desperately in need. And at the start let us get quite plain that it is about *God* that we are talking. The clergy and the laity of the Christian Church need, more perhaps than anything else, to be convinced of the *deity* of God. For it is a persistent temptation for religiously-minded folk to think that God is solely a *religious* concept. By this we mean that we tend to think of him as if he were nothing but the object of religious thought or experience, and at worst we regard him as merely adjectival to our faith or our worship. A parish priest once told the writer that a lady remarked to him that he was blaspheming because he had said that God did not depend upon our belief, and that he would exist even today if nobody believed him to exist!

Now it is fundamental to our Christian heritage to assert the absolute priority and independence of God. He alone is real: he is *ens realissimum*, the one uterly real being, upon whom all else depends, without whom nothing else would exist, who is himself from all eternity and to all eternity. He is the everlasting substantive. And that truth, initially, is a great and wonderful help to man in his need, although it is a truth quite independent of man's need. "The Lord is king, be the earth never so unquiet."

What, then, do we mean by God? We mean the God who is "absolute sole Lord." He is the source of all being, the transcendent God who yet is immanent and operative in his world, holding it in being, sustaining it so that it does not fall into nothingness. He is the purposive being whose plan for his world is being realized—through man, perhaps, but in spite of man's evil and wickedness and imperfection if man turns from God's will. He is the ruler of history. He is, in brief, the God of the Old Testament.

Let us be clear here, too. Often enough we are presented with a modern Marcionism, a God who is not the God of the Old Testament but the God of the New Testament alone. In practice this usually carries the idea that "love is God" before we have seen that God exists, and that the truth really is that God is love. It is irrelevant and hopeless to affirm the love of God unless we first know that there is a God about whom we talk, that he is really there, that he really has power, that he really counts, that he really takes action. Otherwise we are talking only about the loveliness of love and the niceness of being nice, which hardly makes much impression on a world caught in a hellish turmoil. The Christian affirmation is that "though God's arm is strong to smite," as the Old Testament tells us, " 'tis also strong to save," as God shows by his revelation of himself in Christ and in those who, before or after Christ, have declared his loving-kindness.

We can then see that it is to man in his dire need that God comes with his saving deed, his mighty deed, wrought in history in the person of the Lord Jesus Christ. God's direct and intimate concern in and care for man's need and the world's travail is not merely illustrated but it is effectively involved in the act whereby the most high God united with himself our poor humanity, and in the person of the eternal Son became one of our race, so that by that act our race might be eternally united with God, empowered by God, given knowledge of God, and endowed with the hope of everlasting life with God.

This is not merely revelation—that is, a disclosing of what God is like and of how God treats men. It is much more. It is God himself in act. We do not see only a reflection of the divine love in Christ; we see God himself acting lovingly in Christ. Through his humanity we both know and feel his divinity. God clasps our hand, God embraces us in love, God unites us with himself in Christ. *That* is what God does: he does much more than telling us things, as if Christianity were a perpetual lecture or a long moving-picture with a sound-track attached, God save the mark! No, it is union, sharing, participation,

oneness with God who now and forever is united
with our humanity, penetrating it, working in it,
moulding it and making it, in love, to be *his*
humanity.

The Incarnation—for it is that about which we
have been speaking—is the unique and once-for-all
action whereby God has more supremely, more intimately, more enduringly, got himself into his
world than ever before. Now he is here, with man.
With man, notice—and with man *as Man.* What does
that suggest? In the first place, that human bodies
are good things, despite their weakness and imperfection. Human bodies, the physical stuff of which
we are made—and by extension, all that contributes
to them and goes to their making and their fulfilment—all of this is taken by God, and must therefore receive reverent treatment and care. The God-
given material world is the God-assumed material
world; and as Christians we are both enabled to
know and are empowered to use it freely and worthily
as ours, because it is his. A Christianity therefore
which fails to have a social gospel concerned with
man's physical welfare, with the just distribution of
the world's goods, with man's whole being and its
development, and with the right stewardship of the
natural world, is untrue to the faith in the incarnate
Lord.

There is more, however. All of man's intellectual,
moral, spiritual work and effort is also taken by
God and is relevant to him and to his will. Our endeavor to think straight and to think through our
problems has his blessing and will lead to him, if we
pursue our task honestly and bravely. But we are
sinners. That is the truth which a generation ago we
were in grave danger of forgetting. We talked about
progress by education, about salvation by character

—and in the main it all came down to the discovery and employment simply of more subtle ways of sinning. By that we mean more subtle ways of continuing in our self-chosen, unorderly, maladjusted, radically inept ways of behaving. We men act like high-grade simians, though we have not the grace to be nothing but decent monkeys. We are created, though, to act like men. We are meant to *be* men.

In the popular musical play *Oklahoma* an amusing refrain occurs: "How can I be what I ain't?" Well, we cannot really be what we are not. But we can *be* what we *are*. And what are we? We are *human* beings, and our society is a *human* society. By the empowering of God, released in the incarnate Lord, we can be ourselves—but only in that way can we become true men and our society a truly human society. In other words, the doctrine of God the Lord, who for us men and for our salvation became man, is both the guarantee and the granting of that dynamic which makes human achievement possible, as the *gift* of God which is given to us to be *our* task, in his strength.

But the life of incarnate God involved the crucifixion. Here is the fact which optimistic western man has been so prone to forget. In our confidence that we could get what we wanted, we forgot that the world is cruciform—so cruciform, in truth, that even God the Son was compelled to suffer and die. Nor is this merely a tragic incident in human life. It is the way which God royally chose. He reigns from a tree. Hence the Cross is both the condemnation of our human pretension and also the coronation of our human possibility.

There is no certainty whatever that the way of the Cross will lead to the same results that other methods might have achieved—for instance, the establishment of prosperity and security for those who believe. The only victory which is certain is through Good Friday to Easter, but not to Easter as the conventional happy ending. Easter is the vindication and the justification of the Cross, but it is given only to faith. As the risen Lord appeared only to those who had faith in him as Master, so the resurrection victory today is a victory of faith. In other words, then, the fact is that although all our human achievements, be they never so grand, are doomed to defeat or disappointment in this mundane sphere, yet their significance and true being are preserved and transformed in God's purpose. The world will end, our little day will end—and it will be as if it had never been. Hence the notion that the Kingdom of God can be built up on this earth is not only untrue to the New Testament but false to the facts about human life and the natural world in which we live. Yet our struggle to create a new order, to make life nobler here and now, is blessed and lightened by the equally true fact that in this fashion we make a *via* fit for the sons of men as they move towards their true *patria* which is God himself, to abide eternally with God in that intended destiny where God himself reigns eternally. The social gospel, the struggle for better conditions of life here and now, is our task because the ways of this world have been trodden by God the Son, who has thereby made them a way for himself who is the Way.

Now we are perhaps prepared to see that the doctrine of God is of supreme importance because it is by way of saying that what men do matters, what they are matters, what they shall be matters. To men who wonder "if it is all worth while," the doctrine of God says that it is worth while in very truth, because God has prepared for men a destiny of which this world is but the antechamber. Yet, the world here and now is good, it says, because God made it and because he comes into it. But the world is not the final good, because it cannot contain nor can it express the ultimate truth about God and his will. The final good is God's heavenly kingdom alone, where our human desires and hopes may be fulfilled, the partial goodness of this world perfected, and the creation may find its *end* in him.

While we are here, in this vale of our soul-making, we are here to do God's will and to realize our true selves, to become men and to make our society a true human society. Our every action, our every thought, our every personal and social response will play its part, large or small, in this great purpose. We shall be judged by the part we have played, large or small, according to our capacity. That is the ineluctable fact. To it we must be adjusted, with it we must be integrated. That *is* salvation. For if we are not so adjusted, so integrated, we are on the way to increasing disorganization and disorder, personally and socially; and *that* is the road to hell. Hell is the state of disintegration. But there is also the possibility of life in God, in the Church, which is the intimation, the earnest, the first-fruits, of the supernatural order of charity, present here in this world and claiming our allegiance. We are citizens of that order, as we are also citizens of the City of Man. We are amphibians in this double sense, living not only in the two worlds of spirit and sense, but living also in the City of God and in the City of Man. St. Augustine saw that long ago, and he worked out a philosophy of history according to that insight.

To us is given the same task—not only as thinking men and women, but as men and women who must act. Faith in God, supreme reality and ultimate source of all being and life, creator and lord, who for us men lived with us as Man to unite us with himself, who has given us the Holy Spirit whereby we respond, as sharers in the divine life, to the action of God upon us—this faith in God is not only "the soul's divine surmise," in Santayana's phrase. It is also the soul's only hope as it is the soul's supreme response to the God who, having made us for himself, will not let us rest, nor our world rest, until both have found their meaning in him.

6. THE ONE HOLY CATHOLIC CHURCH AND CHRISTIAN UNITY

There can be no doubt that Anglican Catholics, of whatever "stripe," seem to many to occupy a peculiar place in movements towards Christian unity. Their attitude seems to be ambiguous, for they strongly advocate the unity of Christendom, yet they appear to hold back from certain actions which to large numbers of Christians appear necessary if unity is to be achieved. Especially is this true in the matter of the ministry, with the nature and function of the episcopate as the chief point of division. In any event the attitude of Catholics in the Anglican Communion is frequently misunderstood, their sincerity is sometimes considered to be doubtful, and their generosity of spirit is often questioned.

This essay is an attempt to speak as an Anglican —for the writer is himself convinced that to be an Anglican means to be a Catholic in doctrine, discipline, and worship, although doubtless as a member of a "reformed" Catholic communion—and to speak frankly, charitably, and constructively. It is an attempt to present the background from which an Anglican Catholic speaks when he discusses reunion, and against which any judgment of the validity of his position must be undertaken.

Our first point is simply to state a truism. The goal of "ecumenicity," if by that is meant merely a universal confederation of essentially disparate Christian bodies, is not the ultimate goal in Church unity. The clue to the ultimate goal is in the word

"Catholic," whose meaning (as its Greek rooting indicates) is in the first instance "whole" or "complete" or "integral" or even "organic." The goal towards which by God and His grace we are striving or ought to be striving is the realization on earth *in empirical reality* of the true catholicity or wholeness of the Church, its fundamental integrity, as this actually exists in God's intention and in eternal reality. Some kind of confederation, based on mutual understanding and co-operation, is doubtless a step on the way; it is not the end of our labors. That cannot be until and unless we are one, empirically, in the common possession of the historic faith, a common participation in the Eucharistic worship of the Body of Christ, a common manifestation of the life in grace which characterizes the Body, and a common acceptance of the ministry which is authenticated by the whole Church of Christ.

If we take seriously the description of the Church as the Body of Christ, we may properly affirm that the Body is marked by certain structures or "forms" (to use Fr. Herbert's phrase). The Church is not an amorphous or invertebrate entity. It is the extended social humanity of the incarnate Lord, possessing as His Body its own distinctive and characteristic qualities and its own peculiar "culture." Appearing in history from the womb of the older Israel, the Church was marked by a faith in Jesus as Messiah, a rite in which that faith was expressed, and a quality of life called by St. Paul "the life in Christ." No less important was its germinal ministerial articulation, a stewardship of faith and of sacrament which was a characteristic mark of the Church's structure as the Body of Christ.

It took many decades for the naive, unformed and implicit faith of the primitive community to work out into the fully developed Nicene faith. It took many decades for the primitive "breaking of bread" to become the normative Eucharistic offering of the memorial of the sacrifice of Christ. Likewise it took some considerable time—although not so long as some appear to think—for the ministry to come to its generally accepted and normative form. It would be anachronistic to expect to find the full-grown ministry at the year 50 A.D.; but it would be a denial of the normal growth of the Body of Christ to revert to some supposedly primitive form of ministry, even if such could be *proved* to have existed prior to traditional developing and developed Catholic order.

Aware as one is of the problems of nomenclature in the New Testament description of the ministry; conscious of the "Tunnel," as Salmon called it, during the second century, not to say earlier, in our knowledge of development; noting the supposed irregularities at Alexandria and elsewhere, to which attention is rightly called, one is yet compelled to agree with Dr. Burn-Murdoch in a recent book that the *functional* ministry rather than the ministry by any particular set of names, has remained constant in its development, that these functions may be traced back to primitive days, and that the Book of Common Prayer is in this sense correct in saying that "from the apostles' time" there have been three orders of ministry in the Church, bishops, priests, and deacons.

This might not be of such significance were it not for the fact that the ministry is the functioning agent for the whole or integral Body of Christ. This does not so much concern "government" as it does the proclamation of the saving gospel, and leadership in the characteristic action of the Body in the

continued offering of the Memorial of our Lord's
Passion. It is correct and imperative to say that the
whole Body of Christ is the Priest, as being the Body
of Him who is Priest. On the other hand it is inherent in our conception of the Church that the ministry functions *for* that Body, by the Body's appoint-
ment and on its behalf, although never with any
rights *of its own* as a ministry. The ministry is the
essential sacramental *exteriorizing* of the inner or
spiritual apostolicity or *sentness* of the Body of
Christ. The function of the bishop or chief pastor, in
that context, is to insure to finite, time-and-space-
bound man, that continuity of Christian "type," that
identity of evangelical truth, and that unity in fellowship at the Lord's Table, which are of the essence
of whole or "Catholic" Christianity.

The only meaning and purpose of the ministry,
then, is this: to act as the historically persistent
functional and representative agency of the Body of
Christ, to which alone belong both Gospel and Sacraments. The perpetuating of this functional and
representative ministry, on behalf of the Body of
Christ, is a task which the episcopate has performed
since the days when the Church, like a child in its
early years, was finding itself, laying down the pattern for its future behavior, and striking out the
lines along which it would grow and expand. It
would be a blasphemy of the Spirit religiously, as
well as an attempt to reverse the time-process historically, to go back on this reality.*

This is why one who might be called a defender
of dynamic Catholicism must yet insist on the apos-

---

*This position is developed at length and in detail in the
writer's *Bohlen Lectures for 1945* published under the title
His Body The Church.

tolic ministry, with the episcopate as the steward of orders, not as a matter of convenience only, but as an intrinsic element in the fundamental theological structure of the Body of Christ. Here we have a growth and a development of the *given*, as von Hügel would have said; we do not have the devising of a new Christianity for a new day. It is *non nova sed nove*, in the fine phrase of St. Vincent of Lerins. There can be and must be further development, such as the democratizing of the episcopate as a governing body, but the logic of the life of the Church as the Body of Christ forbids us to deny or reject the historic tradition of Christianity.

This is far from a mechanical or legalistic notion. The analogy has been an organic one—a living Body with its established structure and its given ways of behaving. The position is based on a totally sacramental conception of the nature of the Church, as well as of man himself—strange body-mind complex that he is, dependent on sensible things for his knowledge of spirit or value or idea, living by and with and on tradition even when he seeks to shatter or remold it. This view of the ministry is not adventitious or accidental; it is essential to the total world-picture, to the Christian faith, and to historic "churchly appurtenance."

What, then, of the way to the full goal, which (as we have said above) is the empirical expression of the actual Body of Christ as it is eternally and in God's divine intention? For one who takes such a view, it is apparent that such an empirical unity in its true sense cannot come until in each aspect of its integral and whole life, with whatever differences of approach and understanding, the Body expresses itself as one in faith, in worship, in life, and in ordered ministry. But what are some considerations along the way?

First, let us never forget that our Roman Catholic brethren are part of the picture. There is much that one could say at this point; suffice it to remark that there is little to be said for those who discuss reunion and the ecumenical goal, omitting to take into account the strong Christain faith, mixed with whatever error; the right emphasis in Christian worship; and the continued production of lives fragrant with holiness, to be found in the Roman Catholic Church, not to speak of its inevitable place in any truly "ecumenical" Christianity. To the Roman Communion, we must add the Eastern Orthodox Churches. So we cannot agree with any movement which amounts to what has been called "pan-Protestantism." The bringing into a single body of all Protestant Christianity is a very desirable and necessary step. But it is possible that in our zeal we may do harm. Co-operation on all possible levels, by all Christian groups, is helpful provided it does not overlook or minimize the peculiar traditions of each body, Catholic or Protestant. As Anglicans, we believe that the Anglican Communion has its own peculiar and valuable tradition, linked as it is with Reformed Christianity on the one hand and with Rome and Constantinople on the other. Hence, we must agree with John S. Higgins' remark in a recent number of the *Anglican Theological Review:* "Local reunions which endanger the integrity of the Anglican branch of Christ's Holy Catholic Church may have the ultimate effect of retarding the whole ecumenical movement."

We cannot subscribe to Dr. Theodore O. Wedel's statement that Anglicanism is evangelical in faith and catholic in worship and polity. Neither can we agree with Dom Gregory Dix, who in *The Shape of the Liturgy* says precisely the reverse. The specific

genius of Anglicanism in faith and worship and
polity is that it maintained through the vicissitudes
of the Sixteenth and Seventeenth centuries, and still
maintains, the main Catholic position but with due
recognition of the place and importance of the evangelical strain. Because it went through its own peculiar reformation, the Anglican Communion has its
link with Reformed Christianity of other origins; its
misery, as its grandeur, is that it can forget neither
its Catholic heritage nor its Reformed character.

This means that the Anglican Communion is
bound to participate in all aspects of the ecumenical
movement, coöperating in Christian action, playing
its full share in conferences and discussions, working towards theological renewal and understanding.
It does not mean immediate mutual acceptance of
ministries or immediate inter-communion; that
would deny its particular stewardship, its *raison
d'être*. Because this cannot at present be done, the
Anglican will be in pain and anguish. But he can
believe that loyalty to his communion's particular
genius will accomplish more in the long run and that
the empirical realization of the unity of Christ's
Body, when by God's providence it comes, will be
greater and richer because he has been loyal to the
truth as he saw it. Expediency is not the rule of life;
above all, it cannot be the rule for "ecumenical"
Christian thought and action. Principle is the rule;
and for principle we must sometimes sacrifice our
cherished desires and our immediate happiness.

Perhaps something should be said about the discussions in which the Episcopal Church is at present
engaged. We do this with hesitation, for we have
been unable to agree with or approve the kind of
argument used by many who share our own theological views, while we have also been unable to accept

the several proposals that have been put forward
for a united communion. Our single point is that our
first and most important task is a deepened theological understanding and a greater fellowship in the
immediately obvious areas. Until these are achieved,
it would be harmful rather than helpful to move
along other lines. In the final event, some plan for
achieving the outward expression of Christian Catholicity, not totally unlike the *original* South India
Scheme, may be devised. If it is, our hope is that it
will be less vague and theologically inept than that
scheme *now* seems to be. In any case, this sort of
thing should come only after years of deeper, more
realistic fellowship and understanding, with a more
genuine grasp of the wholeness of the historic Christian tradition, than appears to be found at present.

The way to such an agreement, understanding,
and grasp is partly through discussion, partly
through conference, partly through common work.
It is chiefly through prayer. Participation in such
movements as "the Octave for Unity," in which we
may join in a common devotion, each participating in
his own way without raising questions about inter-
communion and immediate moves towards outward
unity, can do much for us all. Here is a realized unity in the supreme Christian action, short of the
Eucharist. We suspect that one reason for the sense
of hurry—which is a different thing from the sense
of the divine urgency of our task— about reunion
proposals is that the proponents do not sufficiently
realize the true unity of all Christians, of whatever
name, in the action of prayer.

Participation in such a fellowship of prayer for
unity should be pointed up and expressed by common participation in worship, to the degree that this
is possible. To join together in direction of the soul

to God is not an unimportant or incidental matter; it is a way towards unity which is utterly fundamental. In this connection, the revival of interest, among Protestants, in liturgical worship is a hopeful sign. For the sense of unity which can be known in worship, and especially in the employment of traditional modes of worship with their rich freightage of devotion, brings us new insight and comprehension as to the nature of Christianity itself.

From this can come a renewed theological exploration. We are being driven back, these days, to the historic gospel and away from minimizing versions or partial expressions of the faith. We can all get back to our confessional position; then *through* that position we can come to the faith which is not peculiarly Anglican or Lutheran or Roman or Presbyterian but genuinely and normatively Christian and Catholic.

It is at this point, and not before, that orders may profitably be discussed. For these are intrinsic to faith; without common faith and its expression in Eucharistic worship, the question of orders is bound to be considered on the wrong grounds. What we need, of course, is a minstry which shall be recognized and given authentication by the whole believing and worshiping community; a ministry which shall be priest offering sacrifice on behalf of the whole priestly community, prophet proclaiming God's will on behalf of the whole prophetic community, pastor tending the souls of men on behalf of the whole shepherding community. We Episcopalians believe that the ministry of apostolic succession, conceived not mechanically but vitally, supplies precisely what we need. But that does not mean, thank God, that everyone must become an "Episcopalian"!

Ultimately, there can be no denominational

Christianity. There can be but the Church of Christ, His Body and Spouse. That is the ultimate goal of our efforts: the realization on earth, under God, of such an expression of the eternal reality of Christ's Church. Please God, the day shall not be too long delayed, nor yet by our hasty efforts made more difficult of final achievement, when there shall be neither Episcopalian nor Presbyterian, neither Romanist nor Orthodox, neither Methodist nor Baptist, but one Body of Christ who is our Head, from whom the whole Body, fitly joined together, shall work for the building up of itself in love.

7. WHAT THE CHURCH HAS TO GIVE

It is R. H. Tawney, the English economist—and a
Christian withal—who remarks somewhere that
those who seek God apart from their fellow men are
likely to find not God but the devil, whose counte-
nance will bear a striking resemblance to their own.
St. Cyprian puts the same truth about Christianity
in rather more "offensive" words: "He who does not
have the Church for his mother cannot have God
for his Father." As that stands, it sounds prepos-
terous. But it may be taken to mean, even for St.
Cyprian himself, that unless we seek God in company with and in the company of the body of the
faithful in Christ—that is, the Church, which is the
carrier of Christianity down through the centuries—
we are quite likely not to find him at all, indeed quite
certain not to do so, if by God we mean that particular apprehension of Reality which is the unique possession of Christian faith.

If this be true, it is inevitable that the Christian
answer to the world's need should be inextricably
bound up with the fact of *community*—a word
which is perhaps overworked these days, but which
none the less expresses a highly significant fact in
human experience. The Church *is* community. It is,
in theological definition, that organic community
brought into being by the action of God in his Incarnation, divine in its essential nature as the Body of
Christ although human in its empirical existence as
a society of men. It is intended to continue the redemptive action of God so that all mankind, or as

many men as will respond, shall be brought into the organic life which is God-manhood. This, to use St. Paul's phrase, is the "en-Christed life." And in order that the life in Christ may have continuity and identity, observable and describable in human terms, it is organizationally and institutionally embodied in that phenomenal reality which we call "the church militant on earth," although its proper eternal reality is far greater and much wider than any such earth-bound institution might appear to signify.

It is the One, Holy, Catholic and Apostolic Church. *One*, in that it is rooted radically in the unity of the God-Man Jesus. *Holy* in that it is separated from "the world" (which means human society in its purely secular and mundane orientation) to the service of God, to the end that it may bring that world to him. *Catholic*, in that it is an integral organism with an interplay and interpenetration of faith, worship, order and life-in-grace, available for all men and adequate for all men. *Apostolic*, in that it is sent from God through Christ to do his work among men, and in its concrete actuality is a divinely established organism whose inner life is God-in-Christ. This is the Church, the *Una Sancta*. Anything less or anything other is not the picture of the Church as the historic Christian faith has painted it.

Now we do not wish to shirk the horrible fact that the Church as we look at it now does not resemble, fully aproach, perhaps even approximate, the description we have just given. It is shabby, divided, in error; it is often prone to sin, at least in its members and in its organizational pretensions and pride. But this is because the Church *empirically* considered, fails to *be* the Church in its proper sense as the Body of Christ; fails, that is, to realize its essential nature. Therefore in its members and by its members it is bound to be less than it should be, less in fact than it actually is in its true reality.

Nor is this a mere playing with words. It is, on the contrary, part of the faith in the Incarnate God and his continuing with us in the "mystical Body," that the Church which is the Body of Christ shall take to itself sinful, weak and erring humanity, and that it shall not miraculously and instantaneously make them over, either individually or in their corporate groupings, into the perfected vehicles for God's will; but that it shall so work in them and through them that by their free human response they become *more* fit (but never *perfect*, in this world of finite things) vehicles, prepared for the perfected life beyond death, in the Church which is "expectant" and "triumphant." Those who expect the empirical institutional Church to be perfect are in the wrong on two counts: they have failed correctly to understand the nature of this finite world, and they have failed correctly to understand the nature of the Holy Catholic Church.

This does not amount, however, to an extenuation of the serious and often appalling imperfection of the empirical Church, nor of the not so often mentioned inadequacies, superficialities, banalities and trivialities of our particular parishes. These are bad; they could be better—shame upon us that we do not make them so! But it does explain our continued imperfection, even when we have done our best; for this, in truth, amounts simply to the fact that we cannot expect to get everything suitably eternalized in this temporal sphere. Men remain men, even in the Church. That is, they are not entirely without temptation to pride, to selfishness and to self-seeking, not entirely removed from their finitude of

judgment and understanding and action. Even the
clergy are men! Ordination does not remove them
from the sphere of human action, although doubtless
many think it does and treat those of us who are in
the ministry accordingly!

What then does the Christian Church, so conceived, have to give to the world in its need, to men
in their travail? We are not concerned here to discuss the Church's programs and policies. We are concerned to stress what the *fact* of the Church, the
simple reality of its existence in this world, its concrete actuality and presence with us, gives to the
world and to men. This is something often overlooked. But we ought to be ready to say that it is a good
thing that there is a Church, a community such as
the Church even in its present imperfection. It
makes a difference and it means something that
there is such a thing—and we ought to make that
truth clearer than we have been accustomed to do.

What the Church does have to give, by its mere
existence, is threefold. It is life-in-union; it is life-in-
charity; it is life-in-God. In a sense these three are
one, subsumed in the last of the chain. But in another sense they are different one from another, or
at least are differentiations within a single theme.
Let us amplify this, considering each of the points
separately.

Life-in-union is something which every man
seeks. None of us lives unto himself; none of us can
do so. Even the most anti-social of us, the psychologists say, are such precisely because we have been
rejected from fellowship and are seeking it in a
perverted fashion. We are *made* for union—physiologically, so that our physical and biological drives
are sexual; psychologically, so that our entire behavior may be described, not adequately but with rea-

sonable precision, in terms of extroversion or its polar yet ambivalent opposite introversion (when we seek the *other* in our selves, having been rejected by the *other* outside us) ; spiritually, so that we seek to link ourselves in fellowship with those with whom we live, trying to enter into their lives and make them one with our own. The success of the corporative states, with all their evil, is explained along these lines. In place of the "rugged" but absurd individualism of western society, they offered men fellowship and mutuality.

But whereas human associations and communities tend to be united either for improper ends or at superficial levels, or without mastering the whole man, the Christian life-in-union gives to men that enduring community which is neither at the mercy of circumstance nor obtainable by ephemeral human association. This is because the Christian life-in-union is grounded in the very being of God himself, in the act of God in Christ, and is thus an ontological reality. Church suppers do not adequately express what we mean, although they have their place; Holy Communion in the risen life of the Lord Jesus does express it. Conferences, valuable as they are, do not express what they mean; the unity of men as they kneel before God, self-given in his act of self-sacrifice, does express it. Here is the point, then, at which the life-in-union for which men strive can be found. And it can be found already and concretely established in the world, not so much to be sought after as to be appropriated because it is *already given* by God in Christ through the mystical Body which is the Church.

Again, men are made for life-in-love. This also is true physiologically and psychologically, as scientific study has disclosed, as the Freudians have made clear, and as literary men like D. H. Lawrence (despite their particular aberrations) have shown us. Spiritually, men have no other end than "to love and be loved." We cannot avoid or evade this fact. And we do well to remember that even hatred is a violent repulsion from men which is in deepest truth nothing other than a defeated, hurt, rejected outgoingness which (because rejected) recoils on itself. Lust, in similar fashion, is that misdirection of desire for fulfilment in love which leads men to act inordinately to obtain what we all, always, rightly, want—namely, to lose ourselves in *another* and so to find ourselves again, enriched by that *other*.

This strong human urge, which in its merely human expressions is frustrated and lost, finds its right fulfilment in the Christian life-in-charity. Here it is possible for men, in the Body of Christ, to let themselves go, if you will; to "go out on a limb" in self-giving love to the brethren; to be transformed through "the expulsive power of a new affection" so that we love in Christ and love the brethren for his sake. Once more, it is not the love after which we strive that is here shared; it is the love which is self-given and from above, the supernatural charity that "en-Christs" men and "en-graces" them. They love because he first loved them. And it can be love without that caution and detachment which are probably needful in the specifically psychiatric concerns; it *must* be without them, else it misses that total identification with the *other* which is the Christian's by gift.

Life-in-God, the last of our differentiations, is in one sense simply another way of stating what has already been indicated about life-in-union and life-in-charity. But it is more in that it insists that the life so known and the love so experienced are a participation in the life of God himself. The Johannine insistence on the reproduction of the life of the Blessed Trinity in the believer—his actual sharing in the vital movement of that life—is a fact too deep and too real in Christian experience to be overlooked or minimized. The community of the Christian Church, the love which floods men when they let themselves go in the fellowship, is not ephemeral or mundane; it is the stuff of God himself. And it is beyond all easy description precisely because each one of us knows it in his own peculiar and personal way. Hence each makes his own distinctive contribution to, each receives his own distinctive share in, the life-in-God.

It is this thing, life-in-God which is life-in-union and life-in-charity, that is the secret of Christianity. Christianity is not belief alone, although it *is* that. It is not ethical endeavor alone, although it is that too. It is much more than these but inclusive of these and of much else, for it is community given to us by God, purging us of our wrong centering and restoring us to our true place in the scheme of things.

But that is not to say that in our world, finite as it is, the reign of supernatural charity, which is life-in-union and hence life-in-God, can ever be fully realized. Yet this is God's world; we dare not act as if the state or any other secular means of social adjustment were "of the devil." God has placed us, who are finite beings, in a world which is finite. That fact "fences us in." We must recognize it, accept it not grudgingly but gladly, make terms with it, and thereby and therefore do our utmost to work out such plans as will bring as much of God's final justice into our relative justice, of his infinite charity into our poor loving, as is possible at any given time or at any given place.

On the other hand, it is characteristic of man—as Mr. Bing Crosby reminded us a few years ago in a very different connection!—that he cries out, "Don't fence me in . . ." He wants the completeness of self-giving, the completeness of union, the completeness of life and love. He wants to "go all out," as Mallory and Irvine on Mount Everest. He wants more than than this finite world can ever give him. It is true that sin comes from his overweening pretension to be or to get more than he can be or can have as a man. But it is also true—and we are sometimes in danger of forgetting it—that it is only when he tries to "go all out," in those ways which are true to his essential God-given humanity, his true norm and his humanity as it is in God's intention, that he is the child of God.

Man's perversions and inversions are not utterly depraved violations of an arbitrary divine *fiat*. They are violations of man's own nature. In that sense they are disobedience to the God who has created man and whose intention for man is exactly that he shall be *man*. Hence in the orthodox theology innocence preceded the fall; the myth states the truth. Man is a creature, intended by God to be true to himself as man: that is, to live in and for others, for God in and through others and for others in and through God, in real community, in real charity. That possibility, supremely, is what the Church as the Body of Christ has to give to this our needy world.

How this profound conception is to be implemented in practice it is not for the theologian to say. But one theologian would say, humbly and as one speaking outside his field and with little parochial experience, that unless some genuine awareness of what has here been sketched is in the hearts and minds of our church leaders and our parish clergy, and from them made vital to our church people, they will never do the one thing that is so necessary—which is to make the Church and the parishes within it living realities, so that each congregation shall be a living Body of the living Christ, and in that way a health-giving because it is a life-giving, love-giving, God-giving reality for the men and women and little children whom our blessed Lord and Savior so dearly loves and to whose narrowed mundane existence he would bring, through his Body the Church, a dignity, a courage, a meaning, and the peace of God which passes understanding.

8. CHRISTIANITY
AND OUR TROUBLED WORLD

It is a truism to say that we are living in a "troubled world." And it is nearly a platitude to say that Christianity is so directly relevant to a world in troublous times that without it we are certain to make no recovery. But what is not always recognized—indeed, what seems to be almost entirely overlooked by many who speak and write on these subjects—is the important and inescapable truth that the answer to our problem is not quite as simple as it might seem when we are told that "Christianity is the answer to our need."

To a large degree this glib manner of solving our problem today is due to an inadequate analysis of the cause of our disorder. It is also due, as we shall see presently, to an imperfect understanding of the fashion in which God and his perfect will are related to the finite world and to man's situation—so far as mutuality of being, as it were, is concerned. But at this point let us concentrate for the moment on our present ills. What in fact is the deep-seated, underlying cause of our trouble today?

I

The fact is that we are witnessing the collapse of a civilization—of our own civilization, indeed. Whatever else may be said, it remains certain that "the shape of things to come" is not going to be at all like the articulated, integrated scheme which we

147

knew some twenty years ago, and which in an enfeebled form survived the first World War. The
world has not faced such a situation as is ours since
the collapse of the Roman Empire—and this for the
simple reason that the movement from one type of
civilization to another in the intervening years from
the fall of Rome to the present time has always been
accompanied by some *continuum* of agreed cultural
values and an agreed social pattern. Now the former
is entirely gone from the *weltanschauung* of the vast
majority of our contemporaries, and the recent
world war with its dubious peace (which at present
we are enjoying!) has accelerated the process by
which the latter is also disappearing. We live "between the times."

The new civilization which will emerge from our
present chaos is variously portrayed. One thing
seems fairly obvious, however. It will be a civilization which will be marked by a planned economy, increasing social controls, invasion of ever-wider
areas of life by governmental agencies. We must be
prepared to meet this, even if we do not happen to
like it. But have we the resources adequate for so
meeting the new order when and as it comes? Once
again, lack of vigorous faith and a genuine dynamic
for living has enfeebled us to an appalling degree.

In brief, then, we are in a situation which is
more radically disordered than the simple reality of
a conflict between democracy and "totalitarianism,"
as the Second War was inaccurately but glowingly
presented to us. We are in the strange position of
witnessing one civilization come to its time of death,
and another begin to emerge into being. Such, it
seems, is the fundamental situation which makes
ours a "troubled world." It is not merely that there
are many things that are wrong, but which can be

set right by a few correct and satisfactory words or actions; nor is it that by the expedient of re-establishing some particular convictions or certain particular beliefs we can make things as once they were. The trouble is much more radical: things will never be as they were. A whole civilization has collapsed, and we are witnessing and participating in the struggle of man to find some way by which life can again be integrated, adjusted, made into a cosmos instead of a chaos. Whatever is accomplished in this direction, the result will be different from that state of things with which we were happily familiar in years past. In this sense, the recent war was simply the last and most desperate stage of a process of decay and death, the final step in a long series of events that both brought about and marked the end of an age and the close of a civilization. From another point of view, it was the birth-pangs of a new order, which will inevitably have some continuity with the past but which will yet emerge as something different from its parent, precisely because it is *new* and because new things, we now know, do occur in the world of historical happenings.

II

Now why has all this come upon us? In a word, because we have sinned. Many of us have disliked this ugly word. But the fact which it describes is even uglier than the word. The modern structure of things which we were pleased to call "our civilization" and which perhaps merited the name, was both based upon and expressed in fact a thoroughly false and viciously sinful attitude to the world and a perverted and sinful manner of behaving both for men and for society. Let us see how this happened.

The last civilization which could make any claim to embody, however imperfectly (and it *was* a very imperfect embodiment, despite its apologists), a balanced and Christian view of man and his world—with due account taken of the fact of a final and directing Reality *(i.e.,* God), was the medieval period. When the Middle Ages collapsed there followed a period of chaos, after which a new and so-called "western" civilization was developed. The Middle Ages collapsed because it seemed impossible, for good reasons to those who advanced them, to allow place in the ordered medieval scheme for the new mercantile, economic and social situation and the new facts of philosophical and scientific discovery, with which the world was confronted.

But the eventual new pattern of "western" civilization was developed with its foundation in ideas of God, of man and of the world which were truncated and imperfect. An optimistic notion of man and his possibilities; an exploiter's conception of the world and its values; and a humanistic doctrine of God: here were the fundamental theses of our late civilization. These three were expressive of and conducive to sin; that is to say, they manifested and involved a wrongly-based, improperly focussed view of life. Man is *not* a paragon of virtue; the world is *not* a place given us to use shamelessly for our own advantage; God is *not* adjectival to man's need, nor is he a "cosmic pal" or "man's great helper."

From these false theses came further sin, in every area of human life. And having led directly to international selfishness, pride in self-development, lack of justice in human relationships, disregard of all enduring moral principles, assumption of prerog-

atives which do not belong to man on any intelligent
reading of the world—having led directly to these,
the fundamental theses themselves broke down.
Then their polar opposites came in their place: man
the slave, either of state or class, because he is a
helpless and hopeless and wild being who must be
controlled; the world as "blood and soil" with which
we are kin; God as tyrant (if we were "religious")
or Reality as sheer fate (if we were "irreligious").
And when these several views, ill-assorted and
mixed, began to operate in life, coming into conflict with the older conceptions, a state of total war
was the inevitable result. We live in the aftermath
of that conflict.

III

It is against this background that we must look
at Christianity. But first of all, it is important to
make plain that Christianity does not spring from
nor depend upon man's need or man's trouble. There
is a kind of theology popular in our own day which
appears to think so. It starts from man's dilemma
and then devises a set of beliefs which will get him
out of the "mess." But the kind of theology with
which traditional Christianity has been concerned
starts from *God* and then comes to man. Mythologi-
cally speaking, we might say that the traditional
"Catholic" scheme always began with God and his
creation of man in original righteousness; it was
only after that had been stated, that original sin (re-
sulting from the "fall of man" as the myth puts it)
came into the picture, with its corollary of redemption. The neo-orthodoxy of our day works the other
way, inverting the proper order of things.

The fundamental Christian conviction stands firm; God *is*, even if man sins, even if man does not exist at all. God is the one supreme, utterly real Being, the *ens realissimum* of St. Thomas Aquinas, the "that than which no greater can be conceived" of St. Anselm. Certainly this conviction is at the heart of the traditional understanding of Christianity. God is no religious concept alone, no merely humanistic *grand être*, no mere "savior of men." He is the one supreme, final directing Reality. The deity of God needs assertion over and over again, these days; and if one were asked, as a Christian theologian, for the first answer which Christian faith can give to the world in trouble, it would be possible to reply in the single word "God"—*provide*d that we meant by God what the Christian tradition has always meant.

In the second place, before we come to consider more closely the Christian faith in its relation to the world's need, we shall do well to see the ways in which in fact an answer *can* be given. Far too much of the time there is an idea that by a few trick phrases and the assertion of a few firm beliefs, the job will be done. There is in the minds of many people the notion that we have on the one hand a set of problems, and on the other the Christian faith. The two can be fitted together quite neatly, and presto! all is well. The impolite comment on that kind of thinking (if it deserves the name) is "Bunk!" The polite comment is that it lacks the dimension of depth; it is all too simple, all too precise. Mr. Whitehead has told us that we are always to seek clarity but always to distrust in it. His profound warning may be useful in our thinking on this matter. There are *no* precise and ready-made answers. The problems are certainly there. So is the Christian faith, with its assertions about God and man, with its aid to man in securing his true destiny. But these two are in a way *incommensurables* in their initial confrontation. The task of the Christian thinker, and of the Christian disciple as well, is to translate and relate what is *given*. His task is to translate it into the idiom of contemporary thought and experience; then he is to relate it to the particular problems of contemporary life. And that is not an easy task, either for the mind or for the life of man. It is not part of the Christian faith, although many talk as if it were, to assume that the Incarnation—God's "en-man-ment" in Jesus Christ— occurred for the explicit purpose of making it unnecessary to use our own heads about our human problems.

IV

What we may properly claim to possess, by way of answer, is an altitude above, an attitude to, and an aptitude for handling, our problems, our "troubled world," which can quite completely change the picture. We have in the Christian faith a new grasp of the meaning of life, growing out of historical events in which God has taken action; we have in the Christian moral tradition a growing set of principles, known largely in their application, which may guide us in our attempt to develop a moral code such as shall be possible for man in the new society which is before him. But these are different from the kind of "penny-in-the-slot" answers which it seems that many are sure ought to be given us by Christianity. Such an attitude, indeed, reflects a "hangover" from the days of magic and superstition —not unlike the popular and erroneous view of prayer as a way of getting what you want when all other conceivable human devices for obtaining it have been given up as failures.

If anyone should expect us to give a precise answer, therefore, he is doomed to disappointment. God cannot be finagled into being our servant; and there is a mystery about him and his ways which no human questing can evade or solve. But we can make assertions, significant assertions, and we can implement these in our living; furthermore, we can be very sure that in our thinking about our faith we do not fall into mere obscurity of expression, confusing this with (or using it as an excuse for avoiding) a more deeply rooted and inevitable obscurity in our thought, because we are indeed handling an obscure matter—the mystery of God as he acts in his world.

Of the Christian faith, then, we may say that its assurances to us are admirably presented in the lovely picture given in the journals of the English mystic, Mother Julian of Norwich. In a "shewing" or vision, she saw the world as a tiny hazelnut, and she asked how the world could be. She was told, in reply, that it *was,* because God *made* it, because God *loved* it, and because God *kept* it. There is the answer—and the only answer—that Christianity can give to a troubled world. God made the world—he is the sovereign creator; God loves the world—he is the compassionate redeemer; God keeps the world —he is the indwelling Spirit who moves through the created order to conform it to his will in ways far beyond our finding out. And because these three are true, human life has meaning, man has dignity, living is a significant possibility.

Hence, to a world which is experiencing the collapse of one civilization and the travail-pains of another, Christian faith speaks, saying that God is Lord, creative, redemptive, inspiring and in-moving. God is Lord, come what may. And come what may, it is within the sweep of his all-encompassing will. Come what may, it bears relationship to his omnipotent love. Come what may, it is not pure chance but in intimate even if mysterious contact with the operation of a divine plan for the created order. As Creator, God is the undergirding Reality and the significant planner; nothing may happen apart from his permissive control. As Redeemer, he saves from futility and frustration every last effort of men, and gives to their works an enduring meaning that delivers them from sheer stupidity and fecklessness. As Inspirer and In-mover, he works through his whole creation, driving it towards its implied and intended goal, never-resting and never-wearying.

God *made* the world. Hence there is the possibility that out of the collapse of the old civilization and from the coming of the new, there may emerge a closer approximation to that righteousness which forever abides in him. God destroys, by methods that are subtle and strange, the evil that men do; he brings down empires and nations; and he has now, through the wrath of men which he has permitted in some personal-impersonal fashion to operate in the realm of human affairs, brought about the ruin of that sinful construction of men's imaginations which they proudly called their "civilization." We have all been found out in our sin—not Hitler and the Japanese war-lords only, but also our traditional British and American systems based on a false *laissez-faire* philosophy, a cheap optimism, a blatant self-content with ourselves and with our own proud achievements. For as Creator, God is also destroyer; the fact that the processes of history contain

what Stephen Spender has well called "the destruc-
tive element" is a proof of the reality of a transcendent God above those processes, yet operative in
them and using them to accomplish his own right-
eous ends. In our self-sufficiency we forgot that *God*
made the world; and so our civilization is destroyed,
—and what is so tragic, our young sons and brothers
were destroyed, too, because of our sin.

But to a world which is caught in a period "between the times," to use the apocalyptic phrase revived by the Swiss theologian Karl Barth, the Christian faith—which asserts the sovereign lordship of
God and his control over history—also asserts God's
love for man and for the world.   God *loves* it, as
Mother Julian was told.   Despite modern perversions, Christianity has not declared this historically
by saying only that God *teaches* us noble truths
about himself in a world which would therefore
seem not unlike a kind of cosmic high-school.   It
declares this by saying that *God has acted in history*.
God has done something; he is always doing things;
he will ever do things.   God so loved the world that
he was not content with being a school-teacher, but
became a Savior.   He so loved the world that he
came into it, and still comes into it, moving as
comrade of men in their common ways.   He so loved
the world that once, in history, he came into it de-
cisively and uniquely, uniting human nature (in all
its limitations) with his very deity in a truly personal fashion, sharing in its experience and living
through it, rising victorious over its limitations and
conquering the selfishness and sinfulness which the
deceitful heart of man had spread abroad through
a fair creation.   And once having so united himself
with his world in the person of Jesus, the Poor Man
of Nazareth, he remains truly one with it.   Our hu-

manity is now a part of the Godhead to all eternity
and so shares (as "partaker in the divine nature")
in a source of power which can irradiate living, in
the here-and-now, with dignity and beauty and significance such as otherwise it could never and does
never possess. He made men members of himself in
a corporate Body, the "blessed company of all faithful people," in which he remains incarnate and
through which he still lives and works in the world.
Nor is all this the namby-pamby notion that "love is
God," which may mean only that it is altogether com-
mendable to be kindly. It is the brave confidence that
God, the ultimate and directive Reality, is love . . .
love of so overwhelming a quality that he cannot be
content until he has come into the world and shared
its suffering and redeemed it to himself. The world,
then, though troubled, is not hopeless nor is it helpless. God loves it. He can and will do something
with it, because he has done something in it, once
for all and everlastingly.

Finally, Christian faith declares that God cares
for and operates invisibly in the world. He *keeps* it.
He is working out his purposes in it; even the collapse of a civilization, with the birth of another, is
part of the plan—although it may not be the ultimate plan for all things. God can, so to say, accom-
modate his purpose to the defections of men; and it
is part of Christian faith to say that in the very
crisis which is upon us, God through his Holy Spirit
is accomplishing his aim, although it may be in ways
past our discerning. In terms of our particular
situation, therefore, the coming social order has in
it something of value in God's sight. It is coming
not only as judgement upon our sin in what we are
pleased to call our "civilization," but because God has
some new thing for us, opening out new ways of

accomplishing in us his purpose of bringing men and
their entire world into fellowship with him and con-
formity to his will.

Precisely how this may be, we are not able to
see. One may fancy, however, that it has something to do with recognizing that in the new circum-
stances and under the new conditions which a
rapidly integrating world provides, men shall have
a chance to live decently in this world, their *via*
towards their *patria* in God, so that they can really
make their souls and not be left as rubbish, discarded by the mighty of this world, to eke out a
miserable and stunted existence. Perhaps that is
what this new planned society, this new corporate
idea, this new "economy by plan," is all about. In
any case, whatever it is, God has a purpose in it and
for it, and out of it some good may be distilled which
will contribute to God's glory and to our nobler
living as his children.

V

The task of the Christian Church is to preach
and to live this gospel of God, without ceasing. It is
not its task to conform to the pattern of any society,
be it "democratic" or "totalitarian" or "corporative." This may mean that the Christian Church
will face bad days, because the Church may refuse
to accept the kind of task which society would im-
pose upon it.

Men may say that the Church is the dynamo behind our social existence, and so it is. They may
say that its faith is the indispensable foundation of
the new plan for society, and so it is. They may
tell us that we ought to be religious men and women

in order to save society from disaster, and so we ought . . . but they will have the order of things wrong. The Christian Church is what it is, because it is the mystical Body of Christ. The faith is an indispensable reality, because it is true and declares God's revelation of himself in Christ. The religious life is essential, because it is man's response to the God who made him, who loves him, who keeps him. When once we have this order straight, we can then go on to say that there can be no freedom, no decent or halfway decent scheme for society, no peaceful world, if God and his righteousness are forgotten. But seek ye *first* . . . and *then:* that is the right order of things.

And so when we are asked to speak of the ways in which the Christian religion is the answer to the troubled world of our time, we must reply that no *religion* can answer any problems, but that the *God* whom the Christian faith proclaims and the *life in him* which it makes available through the Body of Christ, the Church, is the answer. Unless man is related to the source of his being, and unless his society reflects the justice of God, man and his society are doomed.

The story of our race is the story of the discovery of more truth about the world; but it is also the story of God's will revealed to men, and by consequence it is the story of the discovery of more subtle ways of evading the doing of that will, since man is a sinner. But it is even more, we may gratefully add; for it is the story of God's grace, given to men in their sin, so that in the fellowship of the Body they may live in him. It is the story of redemption from sin, of enablement to do his work, in their small way, as his servants in the amelioration of the lot of their brethren and God's "other sons." And

it is, finally, the story of the preparation of men,
one by one and also as a community of brethren in
the blessed society of the redeemed, for their ultimate destiny of life in God, if they will have it so . . .
or life in alienation from God, if they refuse the invi-
tations and solicitations of almighty Love.

This world in which we now live is not an end in
itself; and we shall greatly err, and lead many
astray, if we talk or act as if it were. We are
strangers here, though doubtless for the time we
are *resident* aliens. Heaven is our home; and we are
always and ever restless until we find our rest in
God, as our whole world is hopeless until it find its
true meaning in him. The world—from dirt to
divinely living men—is to be redeemed; and to
man is given the strange privilege of coöperation
in the divine redemption. That is the full-orbed
Christian faith, and we forget it at our peril.

Let us not delude ourselves. The Kingdom of
God cannot be built up by men in this finite world.
By no such earthly city, anyway, would men's broken
hearts be healed. But the Church is the *order of
charity*, the fellowship of those who are being
redeemed, the "ancient and wonderful mystery"
which is the Body of Christ and the spear-
head of God's eternal Kingdom thrust down into this
order of justice which is the kingdom of men. The
Church is here to take this world, which is *of God,*
and to offer it back to him for his divine uses. The
earthly kingdoms may come and go; they do. They
may be better or worse; they are. Yet in them and
by them and through them, God is working out a
purpose. They are meant to approximate his right-
eous will for men—which means simply that men
are to become true men, living in true community,
living toward God who is their true home. All of

us, because we are men, live in the earthly kingdom, at best a pale reflection of divine justice but yet our present habitation and our divinely-given habitation. We live, also, in another city—both we who are Christians and they who are not. We live in the City of God. If we are Christians, we are active participants in the life of that city, sharing its heavenly banquet in sacramental fellowship, shriven by the forgiveness which streams forth from God, seeking to spread the boundaries of the city and to bring others into its secret life. To be a Christian is to be a member of the divine community which is the mystical Body of God-made-man, thus sharing in the power of God in Christ through the Holy Spirit.

VI

I shall conclude this essay and this book by putting these things in a more personal fashion. Am I a pessimist? No, as a Christian I cannot be a pessimist. God reigns, God loves, God cares, be the earth never so unquiet. And it is *this* world, this strange yet lovely world, which God made, loves and provides for; it is *this* world, no other, through which he ever works, in which by his incarnate Son he ever abides, in every corner of which he is present and revealed to those who have eyes to see. No, I cannot be a pessimist. But I must be a realist. The Christian faith speaks to a world that is "troubled": it speaks of a God who is in a world that is "troubled." Hence good can and will be got out of it. But the *world* is not God; and God contradicts and condemns the evil that is in the world, and chiefly and tragically in men's hearts, while he forgives their sin and restores them to himself.

What the Christian faith gives me, among other things, are the courage and the love that make it possible for me, in words from Wystan Auden,

"To love my crooked neighbour
With all my crooked heart."

But above all, it gives me, "as the tears start,"

"The wish and power to take upon myself
the guilt of human action."

To work and to pray to make society more akin to God's purpose of righteousness—yes. But come what may and how it may, to know that insofar as God is my treasure and my hope, my destiny and the path to it, my maker and redeemer and indwelling strength, I may live in community with my brethren and in fellowship with him: that is what the gospel of God says to me. Then it sends me out to my daily task, not giving me "all the answers," but having *already* given me the one answer, which is God himself, known and loved in the divine society which is the Holy Catholic Church.